Redvers Buller V.C.

Redvers Buller V.C.

The African Campaigns:1873-1879

ILLUSTRATED

Sir Redvers Buller, the Ashanti Campaign and the
Zulu War

C. H. Melville

Sir Redvers H. Buller, V.C and the
Ashanti and Zulu Wars

Walter Jerrold

With an Account 'Storming the Inhlobane
Mountain' by James Grant

LEONAUR

Redvers Buller V.C.
The African Campaigns: 1873-1879
Sir Redvers Buller, the Ashanti Campaign and the Zulu War
by C. H. Melville
Sir Redvers H. Buller, V.C and the Ashanti and Zulu Wars
by Walter Jerrold
With an Account 'Storming the Inhlobane Mountain'
by James Grant '

ILLUSTRATED

FIRST EDITION

Leonaur is an imprint of Oakpast Ltd

Copyright in this form © 2021 Oakpast Ltd

ISBN: 978-1-915234-04-9 (hardcover)
ISBN: 978-1-915234-05-6 (softcover)

http://www.leonaur.com

Publisher's Notes

The views expressed in this book are not necessarily
those of the publisher.

Contents

Sir Redvers Buller, the Ashanti Campaign
and the Zulu War

Contents

Preface

The notebooks kept by Redvers Buller while at the Staff College are still extant, and prove that this time was not spent merely in sport and frivolity. They show that he must have not only paid close attention to his lectures, but also read closely in the history of the campaign selected for study, the Austro-German War of 1866.

Amongst his fellow-students were two who afterwards rose to distinction—General Sir William Gatacre, his fellow Whip in the College Drag, and General Sir John Ardagh, who was head of Intelligence at the War Office at the time of the South African War.

Buller did not complete his time at the Staff College. During the August of his second year he was on the Continent, studying the battlefields of the Franco-German War, and fishing in the intervals. Not wishing to have either his work or his play interfered with, he had forgotten to leave his address behind him, a not unknown custom of the Service in like cases.

One night, when in some remote spot, he dreamt that Wolseley was standing at the foot of his bed, saying, "Buller, where are you?" On the next night the dream was repeated. Buller returned home at once, to find that Wolseley had been trying, anxiously but in vain, to get hold of him, and was on the point of appointing someone else in his place on the Staff of the Ashanti Expedition, which was then in preparation.

Buller was anxious not to lose the benefit of his two years' work at the Staff College, by missing the final examination, which if successfully passed would give him the right to put the letters *p.s.c.* after his name, and a definite claim to future Staff employment. Fortunately, the Duke of Cambridge decided that, as far as his professional position was concerned, he should be considered as having graduated.

Buller, however, in the actual event, was never granted the letters *p.s.c*, and his name therefore does not appear in subsequent Army Lists, amongst those of officers who had passed the final examination at the Staff College, or, what is strange enough, amongst the list of those "considered qualified for Staff employment, in consequence of service on the Staff in the field."

CHAPTER 1

The Ashanti Campaign

The Ashanti Campaign marked a very distinct stage in Redvers Buller's career and in his military education.

China had taught him but little. He was a very junior subaltern, and it was not a subaltern's war. More important still, he had not yet begun to take either himself or his profession seriously.

The ten years that elapsed between that campaign and the Red River were critical years. Though still a subaltern, he had had the opportunity of exercising independent command on the "Look Outs," his shooting expeditions had taught him the invaluable lessons of "bush craft," and most important of all he had come under the influence of Hawley.

Promotion to the rank of captain came in the nick of time. The Red River Expedition gave him the opportunity he was waiting for, and brought him into the notice of the most brilliant of the new school of soldiers, Garnet Wolseley.

Then came the Staff College training, to widen his outlook, a training of which only a good regimental officer can reap the full benefit.

In Ashanti he was to see some hard bush fighting, to learn the weakness of the current supply system, and the heart-breaking difficulties of *coolie* transport. Most important of all, he was to be admitted to that inner circle of keen soldiers that collected round Wolseley, long known as the "Ashanti Ring." That "Ring" was much abused by those outside it, and, as is the custom of human nature, most loudly by those who would have been most glad to belong to it. Whatever faults its members may have possessed, there was no room in it for "slackers" or for any soldiers that were not professional soldiers.

The Ashantis occupy the hinterland of Cape Coast Colony, and were then the most warlike tribe in that part of Africa; they had for a long time exercised a reign of terror over the Fantis, or Coast tribes, and it might almost be said over the colonial authorities as well.

There had already been several expeditions against them, none of which had met with conspicuous success, whilst some of them had ended in conspicuous disaster. In 1824, the Governor of Cape Coast Colony, Sir Charles Macarthy, deserted in action by his native allies, was defeated and slain, his head being made an ornament for the royal death-drum.

In the cold weather of 1863-64, a force which was sent up to the River Prah was wiped out by disease alone; "an enemy was never seen or a grain of powder expended." The two factors above noted—*viz.* the untrustworthiness of native allies, and the deadliness of the climate— were as much to be feared in 1874, as in the earlier years referred to, and there were not wanting prophets of evil who predicted that they would again exercise as decisive an influence as they had previously.

It is unnecessary to go in detail into the causes which led to Sir Garnet Wolseley's Expedition. Early in 1873, the Ashantis made one of their periodical inroads into the Protectorate, torturing, enslaving, and killing the unfortunate Fantis who were, at least nominally, under the protection of England.

The troops on the spot were so few in numbers and so widely scattered that they could not do more than hold the various forts on the Coast. A reinforcement of marines was sent from England, and reached Elmina, the most seriously threatened post, on June 12th, inflicting a serious repulse on the enemy on the following day. This had to a certain extent a quieting effect on the Ashantis, but they showed no signs of returning to their own country or evacuating the Protectorate. On the 14th September, Commodore Commerell, the senior naval officer on the Coast, made a reconnaissance in boats up the River Prah, in which he himself was severely wounded; three other naval officers were wounded and several men killed. After this unfortunate occurrence it was obvious that nothing less than a well-organised campaign would suffice to re-establish the authority of the English Government on the Coast.

The first proposal was to send a few selected officers under Captain Glover, R.N., to organise a force of 10,000 men, with the intention of operating up the river Volta (to the east of Cape Coast Castle). This idea was actually carried out, but it was decided to send out in addition Colonel Sir Garnet Wolseley, whom we have already seen commanding the Red River Expedition, to command all Her Majesty's land forces in West Africa, and, as well, to exercise the administration of the civil government of the Colony. Redvers Buller was among the officers originally selected by Captain Glover, on, it is said, the suggestion of Sir Garnet Wolseley. "All the same, I don't think you will get him to go," he is supposed to have added.

The appointment actually given him was that of D.A.A. and Q.M.G. in company with Captain G. L. Huyshe, of the Rifle Brigade, another of Sir Garnet's Red River officers. The special duty with which he was entrusted was that of Intelligence, no easy task, since the information ready to hand was of the most meagre description. In military life, as in other occupations, it is often an advantage to start work on a clean sheet, to choose one's own line unbiased by any previous worker, but it may be doubted if this is the case when one has to collect military intelligence at the opening of a campaign.

Such books as were relevant were referred to, and men who had served on the Coast in various capacities consulted. There were not wanting also gratuitous counsellors, prophets of evil for the most part. "The natives would not fight against the Ashantis." (This unfortunately proved not far from the truth.) "Only Europeans would be of any use (true in part) and they would inevitably succumb to the numerous jungle pestilences" (fortunately a fable). And so on. As to topography, the information available was untrustworthy. The country was said to be an unbroken flat swamp for 30 miles inland.

As a matter of fact, the country as far as the Prah turned out to be a chaos of numerous small rounded hills, intersected by deep gullies. Dense bush covered the whole land right up to Coomassie. The roads were mere jungle tracks, and the rivers ran across, not along, the line of advance, as in the Red River.

Cape Coast Colony is divided from Ashanti by the River Prah, and Sir Garnet's first task was to clear the enemy out of British territory. This he hoped to be able to do with the troops already on the spot supplemented by native levies.

Having cleared the enemy out of the colony, the next step was to make a road up to Prahsu, the point where the Prah was to be crossed, and to construct, at short intervals along this road, hutted camps, so that when the European troops did arrive they should be able to march at once to the frontier, and be provided with shelter from the weather for as long as possible. Sir Garnet thus hoped to avoid two of the great causes of ill-health in the tropics—exposure and *ennui*, the inevitable results of delay. As it turned out eventually it was found possible to construct hutted camps for a considerable distance into the enemy's territory, thus it was not till within a few miles of Coomassie that the troops were at all seriously exposed to the weather.

The success of the campaign was very largely due to these measures. Even with our present-day knowledge of tropical disease it would be difficult to better them, except in matters of detail. Sir Garnet was years ahead of his time in the management of tropical warfare. One has only to compare the Ashanti Expedition with the disastrous French campaign in Madagascar twelve years later to realise to what extent he was in advance.

The third stage was the advance to Coomassie. For this, European troops were absolutely essential, and the government should have realised the fact at the start. Instead, however, they threw on Sir Garnet's shoulders the responsibility of deciding the question after his arrival on the Coast. Sir Garnet was not afraid of responsibility, nor was he a man of slow decision. Within a fortnight of landing he asked for two battalions. The letter was written on the 13th October, but as there was no regular mail service from the Coast it lay in the post office there till the 27th.

Sir Garnet was very anxious that the troops sent out should be volunteers from the twelve best battalions at home, 100 from each, with selected officers, but the suggestion was overruled. Instead, the two first battalions on the foreign service roster were sent, namely, the 2nd battalion 23rd Foot and the 3rd battalion of the Rifle Brigade.

On the 12th September, Sir Garnet and his Staff embarked, at Liverpool, in the West African Company's S.S. *Ambriz*. It would almost seem as if the authorities, in selecting this particular vessel, had made up their minds to test to the utmost the keenness of the officers who had volunteered for the campaign. They had proved superior to the gloomy warnings of those who knew the Coast, of a climate fatal to European life, of death lurking in every breath of air and every cup of water in the African bush: a further test was necessary, so bad food, berths with the paint on them only twelve hours old, bilge water oozing through the cabin floors, bad smells below, and sea water above (for the *Ambriz* was flush-decked) were inflicted on them.

Buller, on the 19th September, writes to his sister:

I am rapidly relapsing into a state of inanition from want of grub. 'Confound the African S.S. Company' is entered as an anathema in my diary and my memory.

16

However, he gives the ship the character of a good sea boat, and looks forward to a good feed at Madeira, where he landed soon after safe and sound except for the loss of his only hat overboard:

So, I have to land in a red nightcap. I hope not to be taken up as a '*bonnet rouge*'—perhaps as I have neither the *collet noir* nor the *perruque blonde* deemed necessary, '*quand on conspire*,' I may escape this time.

Eventually, on the 29th September, the *Ambriz* reached Sierra Leone, where Sir Garnet formally assumed command of Her Majesty's land forces in the West African settlements. Arrangements were made for the raising of native levies, under individual special service officers, Sir Garnet thinking it desirable to get men from places distant from Cape Coast Colony, so as to be less dependent on the Fantis who lived in the Protectorate. These were formed into two regiments under the command of Lieut.-Colonel Evelyn Wood, V.C., and Major Baker Russell.

On the 2nd October, Wolseley landed with his Staff at Cape Coast Castle, and the real business of the campaign began.

Buller's work was, of course, the collection of information. The work was not easy, but he showed:

From the beginning a skill and judgment worthy of a trained detective. The information existing as to the enemy's positions and plans was very vague . . . the numbers of the enemy were but dimly known; no machinery existed for obtaining information; in short, an intelligence department had to be created. . . . Captain Buller . . . commenced forming a corps of interpreters for service at headquarters, and with the officers employed as commissioners to native kings.

The notebook in which he jotted the items of intelligence is still extant, written in pencil with extraordinary neatness and legibility. The work was much hampered by the panic fear which the Ashantis had by their cruelty inspired in the wretched prisoners who managed to escape.

No offers, either of gold to the poor, place to the ambitious, or freedom to the prisoners, can induce anyone to approach the Ashanti camp, such a step being regarded as certain death. (*Buller's Report*, October, 1874.)

On the other hand, the Ashantis had a perfect system of their own, and the Fanti chief assured Sir Garnet that every word they said to him was reported to the king at Coomassie. They derided the possibility of the Ashantis ever being surprised. Yet within a fortnight of landing Buller had organised such an efficient scheme of intelligence that Sir Garnet was able to surprise the depots from which the Ashantis obtained their supplies, in the vicinity of Elmina, and effectually to prevent their getting further assistance from that direction. (From a letter by General Frederick Maurice in *The Times* 1878.)

The attack just referred to was carried out on the 14th October, by a mixed force of Europeans (Bluejackets and Marines) and natives (2nd W.I. Regiment and Houssas), about 800 strong, with one 7-pounder gun and a rocket-tube, under the command of Lieut.-Colonel Evelyn Wood. Sir Garnet accompanied the force to show the natives that he was not merely the Civil Administrator, but also the Commander of the forces on the Coast. Buller's part in the Expedition was, originally, merely to lead "thirty labourers with axes," but during an attack on the village of Essaman, Colonel J. C. McNeill, V.C. (Sir Garnet's second in command), who was leading a party on the British left, was severely wounded, and his place in the fighting was taken by Buller, who himself escaped without further loss than a broken compass vane. The villages of Essaman, Amquana, Akimfoo, and Ampenee, from which the Ashantis had been drawing supplies, were burnt, and the troops returned to Elmina, after a hot and trying march of 21 miles.

The action, though not on a large scale, was of considerable importance, and several useful lessons were learned from the experiences of the day. Chief among these were the unreliability of native levies in action, the necessity of having a large proportion of officers with even British troops in bush fighting, and last, but not least, the fact that white soldiers could without serious ill effects perform one day's very arduous work in the bush. As a matter of fact, there were only two cases of sunstroke during the whole march. The moral effect on the Fanti population was also very good; our friends were encouraged and our enemies seriously alarmed.

On the previous day Sir Garnet had written to England requesting the dispatch of two battalions of infantry, prophesying that they would accomplish their task in six weeks after landing, and producing evidence to show that at that time of year (December to March) there was no reason to suppose that their health would suffer unduly. Later, in view of the possibility of his having to fight a serious action before crossing the Prah, he asked for a third battalion, again pressing his suggestion that a composite unit should be formed. This suggestion was, however, again negatived, the 42nd, the third regiment on the roster, being sent out.

All through October and November constant pressure was kept up on the Ashantis, while at the same time roads were being made up to the Prah River, and huts built at the various camping grounds, for the accommodation of the British troops on their way to the frontier.

All this, however, was not achieved without hard work and sacrifice on the part of those officers who had come out with Sir Garnet. There was a certain amount of fighting. On the 27th October, Colonel Festing of the Royal Marines attacked and destroyed an Ashanti camp at Iscabio, he himself and five of his officers being wounded in the course of the day.

On the 1st November, he again made a reconnaissance in force in the same direction, and lost one officer killed and five wounded. Fever and dysentery also took their toll, and by the end of the first week in November, Sir Garnet had himself to be removed to the *Simoom* hospital ship, and seven out of the ten officers who formed his Staff were on the sick list. Buller did not escape, and was removed to the *Simoom* on the 25th October. He took the infliction lightly. On the 31st October, he writes:

> It does not hurt and is a good thing over, but is not very pleasant while it lasts; just now I am in the sixth day and entering on the interesting stage of convalescence and, except that when I take up a foot I have a strange uncertainty as to where I am going to put it down, there is not much the matter with me.

He manages to extract considerable amusement out of the doctors, who, he says, are always taking their patients' temperatures.

> I think the chap that scored the highest temperature scored something, perhaps a drink; nothing else could have made them so keen.

Clearly his health had not suffered seriously, for he adds:

> Now I have 'paid my footing' I may consider myself, they say, free of the land.

> During his absence from duty his place was filled by Captain W.

Butler, half-pay 69th Regiment, an old Canadian friend of the Red River Expedition.

On the 14th November, he is back again at duty and writing to his sister:

> I am all right again and as fit as a fiddle; we are keeping an excellent roster, as the day I came off the *Simoom* my place was taken by another officer of the H.Q. Staff, who is down with fever.

One of the chief difficulties of his work was the uncertainty of place names, inevitable with an unwritten language.

> The difficulty is sometimes immense, *e.g.* I was at my wits' end yesterday. There were two places spelt by two different officers Yamakind and Jarcah; I told the general that they must be the same place, which he said was absurd. I have this morning succeeded in proving they are. Phonetically the nearest approach to the proper pronunciation would be Myarkin, 'n' being 'n nasal,' and if you try you will see that they both pronounce into something like that. It is the —— to have to deal with a language that has no written character and as many *patois* as there are inhabitants. The operations that took place while I was on board (the *Simoom*) were most successful, and the Ashantis are in full retreat, but they will not go fast enough.
> They are almost starving, poor wretches, and we have the greatest fear that the starving refugees who come in daily may introduce famine fever among us. . . . Our greatest difficulty now is transport, and we are endeavouring to organise a female corps. They are the natural beasts of burden of the country and carry better than the men, and besides one and a half women are forthcoming for one man, as half the men call themselves warriors (cowards would be more appropriate) and won't work.
> We had great difficulty in getting the Cape Coast warriors into the field (now they are there, they run away from a dead Ashanti) and had to enlist the aid of the women. They all turned out dressed as men and painted white, at least, when I say dressed as men, they had left off the wooden bustle, which is the only difference in the dress, and their beads and ornaments, and they hunted the men out of the town. . . .
> There is a newspaper correspondent here now, by the by, who will probably write some live lies. . . . We are now in the little

20

rains . . . I think they have brought a certain amount of fever, as a good many of us are down just now. However, nobody in this country thinks anything of fever, the first attack is the only long one, and after the twentieth the approved cure is to walk in the sun without a hat and smoke a strong cigar. For me the remedy would be worse than the disease.

The cowardice of the Cape Coast natives was one of the greatest difficulties with which the small band of British officers had to contend. Nothing short of physical compulsion, in the form of the flat of a sword, a stick, or an umbrella, would induce them to enter the bush, and once there they immediately lay down. They ran away on the least excuse, and were only courageous when the opportunity arose of torturing a wounded prisoner. With such allies it is a wonder that the Ashantis, who were brave enough and not without the rudiments of a military organisation, were ever driven out of the Colony. The strain on the British officers commanding native troops was very severe, and they suffered much from fever in consequence. On the 4th December, the Ashanti Army had retreated across the River Prah, and the first stage of the campaign was successfully completed.

Buller left Cape Coast Castle on the 6th, and writes to his sister on the 9th from Assin Yancomassie, 17 miles from the Prah:

I left Cape Coast on the 6th, being summoned up to organise a corps of scouts; I fear there is not much to be made out of these fellows. I had about forty of them whom I brought up, and hope to train a corps of 100. There is an excellent fellow going to command them, Grant of the 6th Regiment. Tomorrow Home, the C.R.E., and myself go on to the Prah to select the camping-ground which is to be the rendezvous for the European troops, who will only march up country in detachments. . . . After that I return to Cape Coast to meet the European troops. . . . It never does to boast in this country, but I am feeling better now than I ever was.

This trip gave him his first experience of a tropical jungle, and he is enthusiastic about the forest trees.

The cotton trees are most extraordinary. The roots begin like buttresses 20 feet from the ground, in fact they are buttresses and not roots; the base of a cotton tree would in section be like a starfish. . . . Above the roots the stem goes up straight and smooth and round, and without a branch of any sort, 40, 50, 70, I think 100 feet, and then the top, wooded though not leaved like a large Scotch fir. I never saw more magnificent trees: there are mahogany, coco-nut, banyan, in fact a tropical forest in all its luxuriance of foliage and creepers. Every Ashanti, if the report of the head of the Intelligence Department is to be believed (?), has now fled across the Prah, and the great question for us is, What will the King of Coomassie do—will he fight, or will he sue for peace? or—for as you know there are always three courses, according to Mr. Gladstone—will he blow himself up? I rather incline to the last and first as most likely to happen in combination.

It may be said here that the native scouts about which Buller was so doubtful turned out a great success. Their numbers were eventually raised to 250, and under the command of Lieut. Lord Gifford, of the 24th Regiment, they did excellent work, especially during the last advance on Coomassie. The next letter is dated 31st December, again from Assin Yancomassie. In the meantime, he had returned to the Coast and joined Sir Garnet, who was now leading his European troops up country for the actual business of the Expedition.

We are on the march upcountry, I mean the whole Headquarter Staff, Sir Garnet included. We are followed up the road by the Naval Brigade, and the three European regiments follow in succession by half a battalion a day, so we shall soon have a large party at Prahsu. On the 15th the general advance on Coomassie is to begin, but I hope, I only hope as yet, but I shall not give up the fruition of my hopes without a struggle, that Sir G. will let me go ahead with a small reconnoitring party on the 4th or 5th, as at present we have not the least idea where the Ashantis have got to.

In any case I suppose we advance on the 15th. I think, bar unforeseen accidents, that we ought to be back at Prahsu on the 20th of February, and *en route* for England about the 20th March at the latest, and very glad I shall be to shake the dust of the country off my feet. . . . You would laugh did you see the Headquarter Staff on the march. We are a considerable army— 11 officers, 4 soldiers, orderlies and clerks, general's bodyguard of 15 armed police, 26 servants, and 78 carriers. Most of us walk, Baker and Greaves, two short stumpy men, are transported in a hammock, and the general is dragged by eight men in a light Yankee carriage, the State chariot of His Excellency who rules the destinies of the Gold Coast. The road is not good, the swamps are very roughly corduroyed, and altogether it is a difficult process to get the general along. . . . This part of the road is very pretty if it was not so 'same'; you pine for an open bit. Shut in everywhere with the eternal green, one loses one's appreciation of the richness of the foliage and luxuriance of the growth. I am afraid I have been very remiss in wilting lately, but Baker and Huyshe have both been down and I have been let in for rather a piece of work. The great ambition of my heart is that now the European troops have come out, and our hands are strong enough for anything, we may find that we can make peace without them. Of course it would be a great sell for us, but it would be a great *coup* for Sir Garnet, and he is so charming that he deserves any luck that comes to him. . . . Personally I am very fit, I am walking my 10 to 13 miles a day and skylarking all the day after, with the greatest satisfaction to myself; but then you know the nastiest part of this country is that, well as you may be when you go to bed at night, you may be unable to get out of bed in the morning. . . .

I stopped my letter to open the mailbag which has brought us most unwelcome news: poor dear Charteris' death we had heard of just before we left and deeply grieved over it, he was such a nice fellow and had endeared himself to everybody; now this mail tells us of the death of another of the original *Ambriz* lot—poor Townshend of the 11th, a right good fellow and a capital officer. He will be a great loss to his regiment. Verily this is a beastly climate.

Here there comes a long gap in the letters. Once the Prah was crossed there was but little leisure for writing.

The British troops (Headquarters and one company of the 2nd battalion 23rd, the 42nd, and the 3rd battalion of the Rifle Brigade) landed on the 1st and 2nd of January, and marched up country by half-battalions. The only hitch in the proceedings was the lack of carriers, and drastic measures had to be taken to procure the necessary number. Meanwhile the men of the 1st and 2nd West India Regiments and of Wood's regiment were called on to fill the gap, and received the thanks of the C.-in-C. (H.R.H. the Duke of Cambridge) for the readiness with which they did so. The Highlanders also volunteered for this duty, but were wisely not allowed to attempt such laborious work. Much of the confusion was due to the fact that supply and transport were entrusted to the Control Department, a purely civilian organisation. Sir Garnet took what was then the revolutionary step of handing over transport to combatant officers; Colonel Colley, who had given up a post at the Staff College to join the Expedition, being his right hand in the task of reorganisation.

Wolseley arrived at Prahsu on the 2nd January, and was met almost on arrival by an embassy from the king, which delivered a message of barely concealed defiance. Fortunately, the defiance was a case of words only, there being no Ashanti force anywhere in the vicinity of the Prah. Instead, therefore, of waiting for the European troops to arrive, the native scouts under Lord Gifford and Russell's regiment (native levies) were sent on to clear up the situation and hold advanced posts as far forward as was possible without getting engaged in serious fighting.

Sir Garnet had fully expected to have to fight for the crossing of the Prah, and the uncontested passage of the river was a valuable gift from Fortune. Quite apart from the absence of casualties was the further advantage that it was now possible to construct fortified posts with hutted accommodation for the British troops in the enemy's territory, thus giving these men the benefit of shelter from the climate for a longer period than had been expected. The more rapid advance that was now possible more than counterbalanced the delay caused by the transport difficulties, and though the European troops were a week late in crossing the Prah they were up to time before they got in touch with the enemy.

The road from Prahsu to Coomassie ran through dense bush for about 60 miles. Resistance might be expected at two places, the Adansi Hills and the River Ordah. The former are a steep range of hills about half-way to Coomassie, the latter a fair-sized stream, large enough to require bridging, about 15 miles from the capital.

Fortunately, the Adansi Hills were not held, and were seized by the advanced guard on the 19th January, another though not unexpected gift of Fortune.

Buller in an intelligence report on the 16th January, definitely located the Ashanti force in front of a village called Amoaful, about half-way between the Adansi Hills and the Ordah River, and gave it as his opinion that the decisive action would be at that spot. Brackenbury warned him against the danger of prophesying, but Buller felt so certain of his opinion that he insisted on its inclusion in the report.

He was justified of his faith, for here the enemy was found on the 31st. The force was now closed up and a stiff day's fighting resulted in complete success. The Ashantis fought well, and for the greater part of the day the British force was strung out along 2 miles of track, with the enemy close up to them on all sides. The casualty list was fairly high for this class of work, about *9 per cent.* Fortunately, owing to the poor armament of the Ashantis, only four men were killed. The transport problem was not rendered any the easier, however, by the necessity of providing for the carriage and defence of 200 wounded.

The only unit which suffered severely was the Black Watch at the head of the column: nine officers and 104 men wounded out of a total strength of 516.

The next day Sir Garnet pushed on to Agemmamu, leaving his baggage at Amoaful, further fighting being expected. The resistance, was however, but slight, and Buller, who had been with the advance-guard all day, was sent back in the afternoon to Amoaful to bring on the convoy, a delicate task which he performed successfully before dark.

Sir Garnet was now within 15 miles of Coomassie, and decided to finish the work out of hand. The bulk of the baggage, with the wounded and sickly men, was left with a guard at Agemmamu; four days' rations were issued, and with the men carrying only their greatcoats and ammunition the flying column advanced on the 3rd to the Ordah. This was bridged the same night, and crossed the next morning. The Ashantis had evidently had a lesson at Amoaful; they still fought stubbornly, but they showed less inclination to come to close quarters, and directed their efforts more to harassing the flanks than meeting the advance. Only in one place, Ordahsu, did they make a real stand. They were rushed out of this position by the Highlanders, and with the same rush "their pipes playing, their officers to the front," the 42nd dashed straight on into Coomassie, which was entered by Sir Garnet at 6.15 p.m. the same day.

The king had fled, and refused to return. It was impossible for the force to stay in the capital indefinitely; the weather was bad, incessant storms and rain, the European troops were reduced to less than 1,000 strong, fit for duty, by wounds and sickness, and the men still in the ranks were suffering in health as the result of their rapid advance in a trying and enervating climate. Last of all the rivers were rising rapidly, and any further delay might result in the force being cut off in Coomassie, short of provisions and ammunition. A decision had to

BATTLE OF AMOAFUL

be made and at once. The palace was blown up, and the town set on fire; and by 9 a.m. on the 6th January, the last British soldier had left Coomassie on the homeward march. The night of the 5th-6th, was spent by the prize agents (of whom Buller was one) in collecting as much of the palace treasure as seemed worth carrying away.

The Ordah was reached the same afternoon, and only just in time. The water was 2 feet over the bridge, which gave way before the last troops were on the southern bank, but no casualties occurred, though some of 42nd had to strip and swim for it. After his sleepless night as Prize agent, Buller "worked with indefatigable energy in passing the men over the swollen streams and river." The rest of the journey to the Coast was uneventful, and the last regiment of the force to leave the Coast (the Black Watch, which had been the first to land) embarked on the 27th February, eight weeks all but one day from the date of landing.

Buller's work during the advance from the Prah had been incessant. He was constantly out with his scouts, under Lord Gifford, collecting information, and having an occasional "scrap." In spite of the hard work he appears to have retained his health, till the taking of Coomassie: by the end of the campaign he confessed to being "somewhat worn out," a euphemism for seriously ill. His own account of the Battle of Amoaful and the subsequent advance, etc., taken from his letters home, runs as follows:

> The Ashantis fought well, but we drove them from their position. After the battle, which had not ended at dark, we pushed on into Amoaful, rested there one day, during which we burnt Becquah, and that splendid fellow Gifford got into a rather tight place. He got out of it, with a scratch, however, and I am trying hard to get him the V.C. Please thank Aunt Bella for being the cause of my knowing such a splendid little hero. I think him one of the most charming fellows I ever met.
>
> Tuesday, the 2nd February, we pushed on again, and with an occasional skirmish occupied Agemmamu. There appeared to be a sort of panic among them, for though we found large numbers in front of us we moved them out of the way without much trouble. We had left our baggage behind, and after fighting my way up with the advanced guard, it fell to my evil lot to have to go back to Amoaful to fetch the convoy. I left Agemmamu at 1 p.m. and reached Amoaful about 3, having posted a few men in each of the intermediate villages. When about 3 miles from

Amoaful I met a runner and escort, whom I had sent on to tell them to prepare the convoy, coming back; they said they had been fired at by Shants from a camp we took in the morning and could not get through. I got into Amoaful though, without seeing anything, but I got very nervous about my convoy. I had fifty armed men, white, and thirty-five black, the latter only for the first 2 miles.

After that I had 5 miles more with only fifty men to protect a convoy of 2,300 carriers whom a single shot would throw into a panic. My luck alone carried me through, for I reached this place at 9.30 p.m., and by 11 the whole of the convoy, the head of which came in at 5.30, was in. We started off the next morning and fought our way to the Ordah, having left the greater part of our baggage behind, carrying only four days' rations and a greatcoat each. This day there were several nasty ambuscades along the path, and it was a treat to see little Gifford wandering quietly through them. We lost though three of the best scouts in one of them. Two messages arrived from the king saying that he would agree to all our demands if we would only stop our armies. We knew the beggar by this time, however, and only gave him the night to send in the prisoners and hostages we demanded before we halted.

Of course, he did not do it, his only endeavour being to get time to prepare war-paths and ambuscades for our benefit. During the night we took several prisoners at the different pickets, who all agreed that we had an army of 10,000 men in front and all round us. We were about 1,800 fighting men all told. We advanced about 7 a.m. after a wet, sleepless night. Of course, as it was the first night, we had left our tents behind, so it was the first night that we had torrents of rain. The Shants held their ground stoutly for about seven hours, during which we advanced one mile and secured a village, into which we passed the rest of our baggage and parked it. We were just in time, for the invariable flank attack developed itself, and our rear-guard received a volley which killed one and severely wounded three men. Had this been five minutes before into the baggage I don't know what would have happened. After this our work was easy. We pushed into Coomassie, the Shants flying before us, and at 4.30 p.m. I entered Coomassie, having had the great luck to get up to the head of the column in time to get in with the advanced guard. I was detailed at once with two companies to the palace, to release the prisoners whom the king had got 'in log.' 'Log' consists in placing a man's wrist on a log weighing over 50 lb., and then driving in a staple over it. I never saw such a sight. Most of them were Fantis who could speak a little English, and these naked devils, men and women, crowded round me, logs and all, saying, 'Bless you,' 'The Lord preserve you,' etc., etc., *ad nauseam*. I tried to catch the king, but he had flown; he was so frightened, by the noise of one bullet which sang over his head that he did not come back to Coomassie, but bolted through the back to a place some miles off.

I was never so impressed with anyone as with Sir Garnet, he was cheery and cool to the last. He sent for me at 6 p.m. and said, 'Buller, is the king coming in?'—'He is at least 6 miles off,' I said, 'and bolting.'—'Very well, I shall loot and burn Coomassie, and appoint you Head Prize Agent.'—'Thank you, sir,' I said, for there is a percentage and the loot ought to have been worth something. At 8 p.m., as we were finishing our dinner, he called me and said, 'Have you got your two assistants? Very well, get them, go down to the palace and get what you can out of the palace tonight. I have sent to Home, the C.R.E., to tell him to mine it, and tomorrow I shall burn the town and return.' I don't think a soul knew of this determination. The next morning, we started back, and have been gradually retiring ever since, as fast, that is, as we could get the stores back in front of us. To give you some idea of what the transport work has been: this place is 48 miles from Coomassie; before we can leave this, we have to send 1,800 loads back and 2,300 have already gone. Yet at Coomassie we were short of grub. No transport is so bad or so difficult as *coolies*.

In a letter to his brother, dated 14th February, he gives his views on the campaign as a whole:

We had rather more fighting than we wanted, for out of a grand total of about 2,000 men of all ranks we lost, killed and wounded, 390, or nearly 1 in 5, a heavy percentage, to say nothing of sick. However, luckily slug wounds do not kill, nor do they permanently disable. So, all our wounded are doing well, and killed are few. Personally, I am well satisfied with the campaign, as I hung out all along (officially) that the king did not mean peace in spite of all his professions, though even now I cannot explain why he sent back the white men before he tried his luck at the great battle.

From the political point of view our expedition is a success also, I think, as I fancy it will be done under £2,000,000, and I hope we shall get a treaty out of the king. He paid 1,000 oz. of gold yesterday, as first payment of 50,000 oz. indemnity, and would not I fancy have parted if he did not intend to deal. We were run hard though in Coomassie. Frightful weather, short of grub, a handful of some 1,500 men surrounded by a dense bush full of thousands of howling savages, and our 70 miles of communications attacked at every point, with our few Europeans going down with fever from the exposure, and no hammocks to carry them.

I shall be very glad to get back home, as I am gradually being got to the bottom of. In this country, I cannot say why, if one is dull or seedy for a day one accumulates that dullness or seediness and does not buck up against it as one would anywhere else. I cannot help feeling that I lose energy daily . . . I have really, though I am dull, enjoyed this expedition, and it has done me a great deal of good, but there is an end to all things, and seeing all the regiments go home before me makes me a little jealous to follow. However, we are to go in a good ship, not the *Ambriz* this time, and that is something.

★★★★★★

Note:—Buller's memory lived long in Ashanti. Twenty-two years later, during the Expedition of 1896, Sir Robert Baden-Powell (then Lieut.-Colonel) found that he had acquired amongst the natives the nickname of "Bully." He discovered that this was due to the fact that he had been seen using a compass, on reconnaissance. This instrument had in the mind of the natives a magic power of bringing about the downfall of the enemy, and was associated by them with the name of Redvers Buller, whom they had also seen using it, in 1874. They transferred not only the name to their new officer, but, as Sir Robert informed the present writer, treated him thereafter with a particularly cheery friendliness and confidence, as the successor of the man who so long before had been, as he invariably was, not only the master but the friend of those that served under him.

★★★★★★

As a matter of fact, Buller was a good deal worse than he would confess, and had to be carried the last stages of the downward march in a hammock, desperately ill with Coast fever.

Like many strong men, when they are ill, he hated the idea of giving way to disease, and strongly objected to being put into a hospital ship. Fortunately, a relative of his, Captain John Hext, R.N., was on the Coast in command of H.M.S. *Argus*. Sir Garnet Wolseley went to him and explained the situation, whereon Captain Hext agreed to take Buller on board his ship and look after him till he was fit to be transferred to a transport.

Buller arrived delirious, not able even to recognise his cousin, and dreadfully weak. He was horribly dirty, the mud and dirt from the swamps and rivers grimed into his skin and hair. He was at once placed in a surf boat and taken on to the *Argus*, stripped, and tubbed like a baby, for he was absolutely helpless, and then placed in a hammock, in as cool a spot as could be found.

The *Argus* had to go down the Coast to the River Volta, and by the end of the three days' trip Buller had already picked up wonderfully, and in a few days was transferred to the *Simoom* transport, which took him to England.

It was a considerable time before he threw off the effects of his illness, and even after he had got home he had several smart "goes" of Coast fever.

More permanent and more pleasant results of the campaign were a Brevet Majority and the Companionship of the Bath. He was also appointed Deputy Assistant Adjutant-General at the Horse Guards. In October of the same year, to his great grief, his elder brother, James Howard, of whom he was very fond, died, and he became Squire of Downes.

He might have very reasonably retired at this time, for he was now a wealthy man, with wide local responsibilities, which he took very seriously. Added inducements were his love for a country life and his attachment to his home, as well as his love of shooting, hunting and fishing. He had every excuse then if he decided to leave the Service and settle down comfortably at Downes, but he had by this time got to love soldiering for its own sake. Hawley and Wolseley had shown him how much there was to be done in the way of reform in the army as it then existed, and he had begun to realise his own powers of leadership and administration, and longed to exercise them in a wider sphere than could be provided either in a country, or in a purely regimental life.

He was a conspicuous example of that large number of men who have at all periods of the history of the British Army been content to do their duty to the State, not for any money return, or for any desire for honour or glory, but merely because it is their duty. Honours and high office came to Redvers Buller, but he never asked for either the one or the other: the former were to him immaterial, the latter desired only as giving opportunity for higher and better work.

Redvers Buller spent about four years at the Horse Guards, as Deputy Assistant Adjutant-General with Sir Richard Airey as his chief. As a junior officer he naturally could not expect to do more than carry out routine duties, and though he tried to instil the lessons he had learnt under Hawley into the minds of the Higher Command, he did not apparently meet with much success.

Sir William Butler, who was appointed Deputy Assistant Quartermaster-General in November, 1875, gives in his *Autobiography* an account of the extent to which centralisation was carried out in those days:

> A corporal and a couple of men could not move from Glasgow to Edinburgh except with the sanction, and under the sign-manual, of the Headquarters in London. . . . The thing that soon became clear to me, holding even a subordinate position in that great congeries of confusion then known as the War Office, was the hopelessness of any attempt to simplify or improve matters in any way. A vast wheel was going round, and all men, big and little, were pinned upon it, each one bound to eat a certain set ration of paper every day of his life. It was not the subject so much as the paper that mattered.

Buller undoubtedly received much the same impression, and it was probably during these four years that he first learnt the necessity of decentralisation, if the military system was to acquire any elasticity, and if General Officers Commanding Districts were to be given an opportunity of learning, in time of peace, those financial duties which they would inevitably be called upon to exercise in war.

This was a principle which he was never tired of preaching to the end of his career.

He has often been called a centraliser, and perhaps in his own office, when he was quartermaster-general, or adjutant-general, he was so to a certain extent. He knew "the ropes" of the War Office system far better than any other man under him, and he probably found it quicker to do things himself than to delegate them to juniors. That is a fault common to all men who have great administrative abilities and who think quickly. As regards the relation between the War Office and the Military Districts, he was, however, a strong decentraliser.

It was during this first period spent at the Horse Guards that he took a hand in the reorganisation of the Naval and Military Club, "establishing it on the excellent social and financial basis on which it has ever since rested." (Butler.)

At the beginning of 1878, Buller was offered employment on special service under General Thesiger (afterwards Lord Chelmsford), who was going to the Cape to replace General Sir Arthur Conynghame. At that time the air was full of rumours of war. Russia was threatening Constantinople, and there was a strong feeling in England in favour of intervention. Buller considered the matter carefully, and made up his mind that the chances were against England being dragged into war with Russia, and so, though most of his friends thought, and told him, he was throwing away his chances, he decided to go to the Cape.

It was probably the wisest decision he ever made, for the eighteen months that he spent on this occasion in South Africa were the real foundation of his fame as a fighting soldier.

CHAPTER 2

Kaffir and Zulu Wars

Redvers Buller sailed from Plymouth on the 1st of February, 1878, in the S.S. *American*. He had many companions on board. Major-General the Hon. F. Thesiger—later, Lord Chelmsford—(on his way out to assume the command in South Africa from General Sir Arthur Conynghame), Colonel Evelyn Wood, V.C., a friend of Ashanti days, Lieut. Molyneux of the 22nd Regiment (whose book, *Campaigning in South Africa and Egypt,* gives a good account of the little-known operations in the Perie Bush), Lieut. Melvill of the 24th (who was to die before the year came round in defence of the colours of his regiment), and several other officers, Staff and regimental.

The ship also carried out drafts for the regiments at the Cape, and Molyneux comments on the fact that these were mostly untrained boys, half of whom had never gone through even a recruit's course of musketry, quite unfitted for the severe trial of bush fighting against brave and desperate savages on ground with which the latter were familiar. (*Campaigning in South Afica and Egypt* by Molyneux reprinted as *Zulus & Egyptians*; Leonaur 2021.) In all probability it was while working alongside these men that Buller learnt a lesson which had an important effect on his conduct at Colenso, and that was the danger of sending regular troops to fight in thick bush before the units had become thoroughly welded.

The Kaffir War, the ninth and last of a long series of similar wars, originated, as had usually been the case, in an intertribal quarrel between the Fingoes (Zulus who had fled from the exactions of their chiefs Dingaan and Chaka) and the Galekas, another Bantu tribe, who occupied the territory east of the River Kei. The quarrel, following classical precedent, originated at a marriage feast, followed, as is the custom, by beer-drinking. The resultant war had already been in progress for five months when Thesiger landed at Cape Town on the 25th February.

There had been considerable friction between the Colonial authorities and the General Officer Commanding at the Cape, owing to the refusal by the former to recognize the authority of the latter over any but Imperial troops. The natural consequence was a complete lack of coordination between the movements of the different detachments engaged in suppressing the rising, which had by this time spread to other tribes: the Gaikas under Sandilli, who had fought against us in earlier wars, and another chief called Tini Macomo, being the most important.

After five months' fighting, with varying fortunes, the Galekas, under their chief Kreli, were driven over the Umtata River, eastwards into Pondoland, whilst the Gaikas, Tslambies, and Tambookies, were penned up in the Thomas River bush by the Colonial forces under Commandant Griffiths.

A speedy end to the rebellion seemed certain, and indeed, on handing over the command to General Thesiger, General Conynghame assured him that the war was over: a phrase not unknown in later years in South Africa.

On March the 8th Commandant Griffiths prepared to deal the *coup de grace* to Sandilli and his followers, but unfortunately, he left a gap in his cordon, of which the astute Kaffir took immediate advantage. He broke through between Stutterheim and Cathcart and reached the Perie bush, in the fastnesses of which he had already fought the British thirty years before.

As opponents the Kaffirs were by no means to be despised. Their weapons were the stabbing *assegai*, short and broad-bladed, and the throwing *assegai*, long and tapering, of which latter each man carried half a dozen. In addition to these the *knobkerrie*, and perhaps a gun, made them dangerous enemies on their own ground, the thick bush, tumbled rocks and steep cliffs of the Amatola Mountains.

They were cruel, blood-thirsty savages, no doubt, redeemed in part by a fierce chivalry, and loyalty which inspired them to fight to the death under the leading of their chiefs. In South-East Africa they were as much invaders as the British or the Boers, nor was their tenure of much longer antiquity. They had exterminated or driven out the original inhabitants, the Hottentots and Bushmen, and they could not fairly complain if they were treated as they had treated others.

Buller landed on the 4th March, at East London, and writes from

King William's Town on the 13th, as follows:

I have now got into harness practically though not comfortably, as I have not got my saddlery, which is a great bore. I was sent up yesterday (Tuesday) to report upon the defences of the main road north; we have had a great scare as follows: The two great fastnesses of the Kaffir are in the thick bush about Thomas River, and in the bush of the Iseli and Amatola Mountains. The latter were believed to be quite clear of the enemy, and just before Sir A. Conynghame left, he reported that the war was over, except that the Colonial forces in the Thomas River district had a few Kaffirs left to exterminate. Well, last Sunday, (10th March), these Colonial forces let the Kaffirs slip out of Thomas River and pass across the main north road by Grey Town and Stutterheim to the Iseli Bush. By some perverse stupidity the Colonial authorities had actually denuded these two places of troops, so there was no one to oppose the Kaffirs, who swept through, burning, killing and stealing, and are now in the Iseli Bush.

General Thesiger has now taken command. He sent me up the road to Grey Town to make sure that it was securely garrisoned. I left on Tuesday, (12th March), at 1 p.m., rode to Kei Bridge Station (you will not find it on any map, it is about 6 miles due east of Frankfort), about 16 miles, slept there, rode the next day to Grey Town, 24 miles, and back through Stutterheim to Kabusie Bridge Station, 14 miles. Yesterday I rode from Kabusie here, about 23 miles, so you see I have had plenty of exercise. It is a most charming country, all open grassland something like the Wiltshire Downs, only that the rivers, instead of running in flat valleys, run in gullies.

Today I am to go out to join Commandant Frost as his Staff Officer. He is a civilian and in command of about 500 mounted men. He is now stationed at Old Kabusie Post, close to Mount Thomas, north of the Iseli Mountains. When I reach him, we shall have all the Kaffirs to the south of us, and I hope we shall have some sport with them. I am writing now, as I don't suppose that I shall have much time for writing for the next fortnight or so, so do not be surprised if I miss a mail.

The somewhat unusual nature of Buller's appointment, as Staff Officer to a civilian, is probably explained by the difficulty of keeping touch between the Imperial troops and the Colonial irregulars. The officers of the latter gave but grudging recognition to the general officer commanding and were very lax in the matter of reporting their movements. This was fatal to success in a campaign which demanded the accurate co-ordination of the movements of half a dozen or more small columns. Buller's position was, in fact, that of liaison officer. It has been often stated that he deliberately chose the position with a view to learning the new art of South African warfare, but this does not appear to be the case. He undoubtedly did learn a great deal from his association with Cape irregulars, both British and Boer, and he was far too large-minded to be ashamed of learning from men whom many regular officers, with his experience and training, would have looked on as amateurs. To the end of his career he never failed to acknowledge the debt he owed to the teaching he acquired from these men, and to that of Commandant Frost in particular.

He made it a ruling principle throughout his life never to be too dependent on his subordinates for guidance. At that time, and for many years afterwards, this was the crying fault of the British officer from the subaltern who repeated the words of command at the promptings of his sergeant, to the Staff Officer who was in the hands of his chief clerk. This danger Buller was determined to avoid, and just as in later years he studied the work of every clerk in the War Office, sitting at his desk and going through his year's work with him, so when confronted with campaigning under entirely new conditions he was ready to learn the A B C of the new style of warfare from any man who was qualified to teach it. His association with Commandant Frost did not last very long, as on the 22nd April, he was offered the command of the Frontier Light Horse. During the five or six weeks that he was with Frost, he took part in several drives, which were but partly successful. The volunteers, most of whom had only engaged to serve for three months, returned to their homes, and operations practically ceased during the last fortnight of April.

The Frontier Light Horse was a miscellaneous collection of men—British, Boer, and alien—of any or no occupation (his regimental sergeant-major was a deserter from the 80th Foot), a force that under a weak commander would be not only useless, but, in Abercromby's phrase, "a terror to everyone but the enemy." Fortunately, they got the man they needed in Buller, though he was not over and above sanguine at the prospect before him. He writes to his sister, on the day he received his command:

Frontier Light Horse

They are in terribly bad order, and I fear there is not much credit to be got out of being associated with them, but I will do my
best; it is at any rate something to be one's own CO. Whatever
happens, I mean to try and make a splash with them somehow.

It did not take him long to get his command into order. Colonel
Lewis Butler, in speaking of this period in Buller's career, says:

There was a stern side to Buller's character, and shortly after
assuming his command he had occasion to show it. Having
had some hard work, the commanding officer gave the men a
short rest, but knowing they would spend the interval for the
most part in a state of intoxication, he warned them to come
to parade sober and fit for service in two days' time. The regiment answered to his call pretty well; one man, however, was
not only drunk but actually dared to abuse the CO. loudly to
his face. Buller said nothing except to give the word of command to march; but, having gone a few miles, halted, and then,
in the most conspicuous manner possible, ordered the man to
dismount, and sent him about his business.
The one example sufficed. Insubordination was quelled forever,
and that it took an astonishingly short time to get his regiment
in order was due to that splendid element of magnetic sympa-
thy known as 'power of command.' The men felt it personally
degrading to do anything the colonel disliked. At a later period,
a man misbehaved. He was forgiven. He repeated the offence.
He was urged to ask forgiveness again, but he was quite unable
to bring himself to do so. 'I cannot,' he moaned piteously, 'I cannot face Buller.' (Butler.)

But though the men dreaded his severity they knew that they
could rely on his inflexible justice; his rebuke, dreaded though it was,
left no rankling sense of unfair or wanton punishment, the one thing
that the man in the ranks never forgives. His men found him acces-
sible to their complaints, and sympathetic to their troubles; he shared
their hardships and was foremost in their dangers.

Wherever the stiffest place was he was sure to be found. In action if you could ascertain for certain where the most bullets
were flying, you could be pretty safe in venturing your last dol-
lar that Buller would be in the middle of it. (*Kaffirland: A Ten
Months' Campaign*. F. N. Streatfield.)

No matter, however apparently trivial, that affected the comfort or efficiency of his men was too small for him to spend his time and trouble on. The writer just quoted speaks of having seen him spend hours in getting saddles to fit properly so as to avoid sore-back as far as possible.

He made no attempt to win popularity, nor did he try to impress his personality on his men, but strangers were often struck by the effect produced by his sudden appearance at the door of his tent and the awe with which his rough troopers regarded him. It was certainly not due to any adventitious aid from dress, for in this matter he was far from formal. He was always an early riser, and used to appear in shirt sleeves, slippers, no stockings, riding-breeches without leggings, and a red scarf turned into a night cap; thus attired, he would walk through his horse lines to see if all were well. One of his men afterwards said, "It didn't matter what he wore, it was enough that he was there."

"Though his men feared him they had a sort of dog-like love for him": thus, Archibald Forbes described the relation of the Frontier Light Horse to their commanding officer.

His first engagement with his new command was on the 30th April, when he led a mixed force of about 900 Europeans and natives in a drive in which three other similar columns co-operated, with fair success. He writes on Monday, the 13th May, to his sister:

> We have had several goes at *Messieurs* the Kaffirs lately with varying success. The week before last we surrounded the bush of the Intaba N'doda Mountain, near the King William's Town-Fort Beaufort Road, and made rather a good thing of it, as all the arrangements came off. We killed a larger number of Kaffirs than usual (*according to Molyneux, 130*), and everybody was well satisfied with the day's work. Last week (*actually on the 8th April, 1878*) we tried again to surround the Perie Bush, that place under the Quilli-Quilli Mountain from which I wrote four or five weeks ago, and our arrangements did not quite come off, and I fancy we suffered almost as much as the Kaffirs did, who I must confess fought well. I got into unpleasantly close quarters with them with some of my new regiment, the Frontier Light Horse, and we suffered heavily, losing both captains, one killed, the other severely wounded, and four men killed and two more wounded, to death I fear.
>
> It was a very nasty place, the head of a path leading down what

they call a *krantz* in this country (which means a precipitous cliff). The cliff went down on each side sheer for about 200 feet; there was a sort of rugged cleft in the centre of it full of bush and large boulder rocks, and down this the path, such as it was, ran. Oddly enough I had rather been afraid of this place, and had made the general promise that he would send a company to the bottom of the *krantz*, which would have made the place untenable, as the Kaffirs could have been picked off from the bottom like young rooks off a tree. By some accident the captain of the company made a mistake, and by another accident Degacher of the 24th did not get to the top of the *krantz* in time. I saw about 300 Kaffirs bolting off, and pursued them, but managed to get to the place with only my personal escort of five men. We were greeted by a volley and we jumped off our horses, leaving them in charge of one man.

Calling up some other volunteers who were near I went for the path. Two of my escort were shot down in a second, but I got right up to the rocks with the other two men, when those rascally 'Wodehouse Pine Blues,' as they call themselves, instead of coming on, lay down and commenced firing at the rocks, and of course at us. This was rather too hot for this child, so as I had no intention of being made a sandwich of between two slices of lead, I came back, losing another man as I did so, shot by his friends. After this we could do nothing till some more men came up. I got up the rest of the regiment, but unfortunately Macnaghten, one captain, was shot dead, and Whalley, the other, wounded. This stopped us a second time, and it was some time before we came again. However, with the help of the Fingoes we got in and killed all the people inside the rocks, about fifteen, not many, but quite enough to make it hot for us, as there was only room for two of us to go in at a time.

Evelyn Wood fills some gaps in the above rather bald narrative. (See *Evelyn Wood, V.C.: the Ashanti, Gaika & Zulu Wars—The Campaigns in Africa 1873-1880* containing *My Zululand Experiences* by Evelyn Wood & *Ashanti to the Zulu War* by Charles Williams; Leonaur, 2018.) He arrived on the scene just after Captain Macnaghten had been hit.

Major Buller reported that there were only thirty Kaffirs immediately below him, the man who shot Macnaghten being in a tree farther westward along the precipice. He explained that most of the enemy were behind a big rock, 40 feet down, a place so steep that you could not go down without holding on, or sliding, so that it was difficult to turn them out as I wished, and he demurred to the inevitable loss of men in the operation. I suggested that it was only the first man down who was likely to be shot, and signalling to Captain Laye, who was on a terrace 200 feet below me, he brought up his company. . . . . I explained the operations and its dangers to Captain Laye, telling him he was to sit and slide down the rock, ordering one of his most trustworthy men to keep close to him. Just as the company, which had extended while in 'dead' ground, approached the edge of the precipice, Buller jumping up shouted, 'Frontier Light Horse, you will never let those redcoats beat you,' and forming himself into a toboggan, he slid down, under fire, which fortunately passed over his head, and most of the Kaffirs disappeared before he regained his footing.

General Thesiger in his dispatch says, referring to Buller's conduct on this occasion:

He set an example of intrepidity and calm courage to his men under very trying circumstances, and though the operations of this day were not attended with all the success I expected, he did his best by his personal example to secure it.

Six small columns were engaged in this fighting, and owing to one of these losing its way, a gap was left in the cordon through which many of the Kaffirs escaped.

The war went on for a few more weeks, and was ended by the death of Sandilli and the capture of Tini Macomo. Buller on one occasion, towards the end of May, very nearly captured the former, having cornered him, as he thought, in a cave, from which there was no outlet beyond those he had seized. Unfortunately, this proved not to be the case, and the wily old chief escaped, to meet his end later by death on the battlefield, a kindlier fate than captivity.

The revolt of the Kaffirs was only the local manifestation of a very widespread feeling of unrest amongst the native tribes of South Africa generally. Of these the most threatening were Sekukuni's people, in the Lydenburg district of the Transvaal, Basutos in origin, and the Zulus, under Ketchwayo. The former had already two years before repulsed the Boers, and more than held their own against some volunteer forces in the earlier part of 1877.

As long as the Kaffir War continued it was impossible to send any reinforcements to the Transvaal, whilst the regular troops already there (three companies of the l/13th Foot) were tied to Pretoria by reason of the discontent amongst the Boers resulting from the annexation. The close of the Kaffir War, however, released the troops engaged in those operations, and, amongst others, the Frontier Light Horse were selected to proceed to the North. Their commanding officer writes on the 2nd June:

> There is a rumour that I am to march to the Transvaal with the 90th under E. Wood and some guns. It sounds to be too good to be true, but it would be great fun should it prove correct.

Wood started on his march from Kei Road on the 25th June, but Buller was not ready to accompany him. In a letter written the next day he propounds the following problem in logistics for his sister to solve:

> If Colonel Wood marches 90 miles a week and has nine days' start, when will Major Buller, who marches 140 miles a week, catch him, and will he do so at all if the total distance is under 500 miles? I trust, however, that Wood will not be able to make 90 miles a week, and that I shall do at least 140, if not more.

He eventually got off on the 7th July, with 203 men of the F.L.H., forty-one of whom had joined up only two days before. He arrived at Umtata on the 19th July, and at Kokstad on the 29th, having caught up with Evelyn Wood on the 28th, so that presumably they maintained about the relative rates of marching that he anticipated. The Pondos had been giving trouble lately and there appeared some prospect of having to teach them a lesson. He did not look forward with any pleasure to this instructional essay, "as they are great cowards and so we are not likely to get any very amusing fighting." Besides, he was anxious to get on to the more important work that the Zulus seemed likely to provide. He enjoyed the march up country and was much impressed by the vastness of the open *veldt*. The march was uneventful, and the only trouble was due to the grass having been burnt up by a long drought.

A fortnight later he is still at Kokstad and writes on the 13th August:

> We are still here waiting for the Pondos, and the Pondos are at Palmers Town waiting for us, and so we are likely to be here for

the rest of our natural lives, for neither side seems likely to give in. . . . At present the rumour is that Cetewayo, the Zulu chief, will not fight; on the other hand, they say that he has actually commenced overt acts of war. I must say that I should like to have just one little shy at the Zulus. People say that they will attack us in the open, and if they do that it would be great fun.

War was still to Buller a game: a rough game, it is true, but one not worth playing unless the other side had a good sporting chance, and was prepared to make the best use of it.

The Pondo trouble came to nothing, and by the 23rd August, he was at Pietermaritzburg, writing:

I rode in here from the Ixopo (pronounced I-click-kopo) River yesterday, just 60 miles. Leaving at 4.25 a.m., I was here at 3.26 p.m.: a good performance for the horses. I brought in five: riding one, my boy riding one and leading another which carried a pack, and my orderly riding a horse and leading my pony. They all fed well, and I have been riding the pony about all day today. Such are Cape horses. That reminds me that I have never introduced you to my horses.

I have now seven. First and foremost, there is 'Billy,' a brown pony, that I bought the day I reached King. Then there is 'Bob,' a big bay horse that I bought in King, very good and very ugly. Then there is 'Blue Buck,' a grey horse that always carries the pack and never tires. Then 'Yellow Jack,' a very good-looking and good cream-coloured cob: these are my four *par excellence*. Then there are 'Dick,' a capital chestnut my orderly rides; 'Skylark,' a fidgety grey that Packe, my soldier servant, bestrides; and 'Philip,' my cook's horse.

These seven constitute my stud, and of course great interest I take in them. Besides these I have two most excellent charming pets, two black greyhounds who sleep in my bed and keep me warm at night, and are generally cheerful and charming during the day. I had great fun at Kokstad coursing buck. I never succeeded in catching one, but we had some wonderful runs, and I got a most wonderful purl, for poor old 'Bob' put his foot in a hole and turned a complete somersault over me. They all thought that I must be killed, but by some happy luck I was not hurt in the least, neither, I am happy to say, was 'Bob.' I find that my journey is not nearly over, for I start Tuesday (27th) or

Wednesday for Lydenburg, due north of Newcastle. I shall have to go round by Pretoria, a journey of 600 miles. The general says I must if possible be there by the 25th of next month, so I shall have to travel at least 25 miles a day to do it: sharp work.

He spent about a month in Sekukuni's country, with a little unsatisfactory fighting which cost him, to his great sorrow, his servant, Packe, a rifleman of the 60th, severely wounded, and a great deal of horse sickness, which killed about a quarter of his horses, including his own charger "Blue Buck," of whom he was very fond. To avoid further loss of animals he was ordered back towards Newcastle, and went into camp between Utrecht and Luneberg to await developments. His time was occupied in recruiting (he had been ordered to increase his establishment by 100 men), procuring remounts and equipment. This involved a hurried visit to Pietermaritzburg, 200 miles from the site of his camp, which distance he covered in about fifty hours. He spent a happy week there, living with his friend and brother officer Francis Grenfell, (later Field-Marshal Lord Grenfell, P.C., G.C.B.) and messing at the general's table.

Meanwhile the Zulu question was drawing to a head. The king Ketchwayo maintained an arrogant attitude, and was obviously preparing his army for war. Two of his chiefs, by name Sirayo and Umbelini, made raids across the Natal frontier, abducting and killing native women, and it became clear that the only way in which a Zulu invasion could be prevented was by forestalling it. The frontier was too extended, and the available force too small, for a passive defence.

An ultimatum was sent to Ketchwayo by the High Commissioner for South Africa, Sir Bartle Frere, couched in terms which it was almost certain that he would not accept, but at the same time expressing the minimum necessary to ensure peace along the Natal frontier for the future.

Five columns were prepared as follows:

No. 1 (Right) Column, at the Lower Tugela Drift, under the command of Colonel Pearson, of the Buffs; 2nd battalion of the Buffs, and the 99th Foot, etc., in all rather over 4,000 fighting men, of whom 2,200 were natives; two 7-pounder guns, one Gatling, two rocket tubes and one trough.

No. 2 Column, at Kranzkop, Middle Drift, under the command of Colonel Durnford, R.E., 3,800 natives, with three rocket troughs.

No. 3 (Centre, or Headquarters) Column, at Rorke's Drift, commanded by Colonel Glyn, C.B., 24th Foot; 24th Foot, both battalions, etc., in all about 4,000 fighting men, of whom 2,500 were natives; six 7-pounder guns, and two rocket troughs.

No. 4 (Left) Column, at Conference Hill, on the Blood River (near Utrecht), commanded by Brevet-Colonel Evelyn Wood, V.C., C.B., 90th Foot; 1st battalion 13th Foot, 90th Foot, Frontier Light Horse, and Wood's Irregulars, etc., in all just under 2,100 fighting men, of whom less than 400 were natives; six 7-pounders, and two rocket troughs.

No. 5 Column, at Luneberg, commanded by Colonel Rowlands, V.C., C.B., h.p., 34th Foot; 80th Foot, and various small contingents of irregulars, in all just over 1,700 fighting men, of whom a little more than 300 were natives.

Lieut.-General Lord Chelmsford was in supreme command.

The 5th column was intended rather to act as a check on Sekukuni than to share in the invasion, whilst No. 2 Column formed a reserve to the Centre Column.

The ultimatum nominally expired at midnight on the 11th January, but Colonel Evelyn Wood had by that time already advanced to a place named Bemba's Kop, on the left bank of the Blood River, about 35 miles from Rorke's Drift, with a view to acting in support of the Centre Column should it be seriously opposed at the crossing of the Tugela.

The Right Column crossed at the Lower Tugela Drift on the 12th January, and meeting with no resistance pushed on into Zulu territory as far as the Inyezani River, where it had its first encounter with the enemy. On the 22nd, the Zulus attacked, and were repulsed without difficulty, losing heavily. The British loss was 2 officers and 8 men killed, 1 officer and 15 men wounded. Colonel Pearson then advanced to the mission station of Etshowe, where he prepared a defensible post, preparatory to a combined movement on Ulundi (the Zulu capital) in conjunction with the Centre and Left Columns.

The Centre Column crossed the Tugela on the 11th. Lieut.-General Lord Chelmsford, who accompanied this column, rode over the same day to meet and consult with Colonel Evelyn Wood, who came halfway to Rorke's Drift for the purpose, with a small flying column consisting of the Frontier Light Horse, Wood's Irregulars, and some picked marksmen of the 13th and 90th Regiments, with two guns.

On the 12th the *kraal* of Sirayo, one of the chiefs who had raided over the border, was burnt, and the succeeding week was taken up with reconnaissance; meanwhile the crossing at the drift was improved, and stores and supplies brought over.

A further advance was made to a hill named Isandhlwana, about 15 miles from the drift, and a camp formed on the 20th. On the 21st, a reconnoitring force was again sent out, the bulk of the column remaining in camp. The reconnaissance met with more resistance than it could overcome, and on the 22nd, Lord Chelmsford moved out to its support, with four guns, six companies of the 2 /24th, and some native troops. During his absence the camp was attacked by the Zulus, in overwhelming strength, and since no adequate measures had been taken to put it into a proper state of defence, the entire force that had been left behind was destroyed.

Information of the disaster reached Lord Chelmsford in the course of the afternoon, and he at once returned to Isandhlwana, with the remainder of his column. The night was spent by this force in the devastated camp, amongst the corpses of their comrades. Early the next morning Lord Chelmsford marched his men back to the Tugela, which was crossed before noon. To the intense relief of all it was found that the small detachment left in the improvised defences of Rorke's Drift had, though heavily attacked throughout the night, managed to hold its own, not without heavy loss, but, at the same time, not without inflicting severe punishment on the enemy.

The casualty list of Isandhlwana amounted to 52 officers, 806 European rank and file, and 471 natives, killed. That of Rorke's Drift to 1 officer, wounded, 15 rank and file killed, and 9 wounded, out of a total strength of 139 officers and men.

The original plan of campaign had contemplated a gradual advance of the first, third, and fourth columns into the enemy's country, terminating in a combined attack on the king's head *kraal* at Ulundi. The disaster which had befallen the centre column brought the scheme to an abrupt end. The tables were turned, and instead of thinking of the invasion of Zululand, the general was now occupied with plans for the defence of Natal, until such time as reinforcements could arrive from home. Time was unavoidably lost from the fact that there was, at that time, no direct telegraphic communication between the Cape and England. The general's report of the disaster had in consequence to go by steamer as far as St. Vincent; leaving Cape Town on the 27th January, it did not reach the Secretary of State for War till the 11th February.

Fortunately, when the news got to St. Helena, on the 6th February, H.M.S. *Shah* was in harbour on her way home from the Pacific station. Captain Bradshaw, in command, decided to return to the Cape, with a battery (8/7 R.A.), and one company of the 88th Foot at that time stationed on St. Helena. He was also able to supply a naval contingent of some 400 men. These reinforcements landed at Durban on the 6th March.

No time was lost in sending reinforcements from home. These consisted of two regiments of Cavalry (1st D.G.s and 17th Lancers), two batteries of Royal Artillery (M and N of the 6th Brigade; six 7-pounder and six 9-pounder guns), five battalions of Infantry (2/21st, 58th, 3/60th, 91st, and 94th), with drafts for other regiments; amounting in all (with R.E. and Departmental Corps and Staff) to 387 officers and 8,895 men. The great bulk of these were embarked by the end of February and disembarked in Natal by the end of the first week in April. In addition, the 57th Foot was brought from Ceylon, and three 7-pounder guns, and one company 88th Foot from Mauritius.

Considering all things, the rate of steaming of vessels in those days, etc., this must be looked on as a very creditable performance.

The news of the disaster at Isandhlwana did not reach Colonel Pearson at Etshowe till the 27th. He was at the time engaged in the construction of a defensible post, and in preparations for his next advance. On the 28th, however, he received a message from Lord Chelmsford cancelling all previous orders and directing him to act in the manner that seemed to him most advisable. He was permitted even to retire from Etshowe, should he consider that post too advanced, and fall back to the line of the Tugela, only maintaining a position on the left bank. He decided, however, to continue to hold Etshowe, with a reduced garrison, sending away all mounted men and the native contingent. On the 30th January, he moved into the Fort, with a total strength of a little over 1,300 white troops and 350 black.

To anticipate, it may be said here that the siege of Etshowe lasted about nine weeks. It was relieved on the 3rd of April, by a column which left Fort Pearson on the 28th March, having encountered and defeated the Zulus at Ginghilovo on the 2nd April. Our losses on this occasion were trifling: 9 rank and file killed, 6 officers and 46 rank and file wounded. Two of each class died of their wounds. The garrison and the relieving column then returned to the left bank of the Tugela, a detachment being left in an entrenched position near Ginghilovo.

It is now time to return to the doings of the Left Column under

Colonel Evelyn Wood. After the meeting between Lord Chelmsford and Colonel Wood on the 11th January, already referred to, the flying column rejoined its main body on the 13th. The next ten days were taken up in desultory skirmishing and reconnaissance, the Zulus, though present in considerable numbers, being apparently uncertain, in the absence of definite orders from the king, whether they were to oppose the British advance or not.

The news of Isandhlwana reached Colonel Wood on the 23rd, while actually engaged in a skirmish to the north of Inhlobana Mountain.

He immediately fell back to a prepared position on the White Umvolosi, named Fort Tinta, and from thence to Kambula Hill, where a strong entrenched camp was formed. Buller was kept fairly busy. He writes on the 14th February:

> I have lots to do and very little to write about. In the saddle for eighty hours a week does not leave one much time for writing, and sleeping, and that is about the amount of riding that I have to do now, for I have nearly 160 square miles of country to patrol with a very inadequate force. However, the result of the work has as yet been satisfactory, for ours is the only column that is free to move when and where it likes, and we are not, thank Heaven, helpless and entrenched, but are masters of our situation.... Everything is out of joint out here now, the general is down on his luck and things are not going well; however, we have plenty of time to get straight in, as it will be at least another month before any reinforcements can reach here, and I am sure that the general will not venture in again till they do come.
>
> It is very hard luck for me that just now when everybody is downhearted, and I should, I feel confident, gain more credit than I deserve for any tolerably bold stroke, that I am so terribly weak in men, owing to many of mine having taken their discharge, on the expiration of their period of service on the 30th of January. All told in camp here, Frontier Light Horse, *Burghers*, and all, I have scarcely 150 men, and deducting from that the number necessary to protect the camp I have not more than 100 at my disposal, a force too small to strike an effective blow with.
>
> However, I must be thankful for small mercies. I have got a good deal of credit for burning a few old huts some thirty miles from here, called the Bagulusini Military Kraal. We had

no casualties, and really it was not much: still, the general writes that he has specially reported me to the S. of S., and every little helps, for if I am to get anything out of the Zulu War in the way of further promotion I must do a big thing, otherwise I have not a chance. Small brevets are easy enough to get, but the plum of a full colonelcy is another matter.

He does not in this letter refer to a smart piece of work carried out by him in company with Mr. Piet Uys, a member of one of the oldest Boer families, and a son of one of the original "*Voortrekkers.*"

On the 15th of February they marched with a mixed force, about 600 strong, to the Intombi Valley to punish a Zulu chief who had been raiding farms in the Luneberg district. The Zulus were posted in caves on the banks of the Intombi River, out of which they had to be driven. A considerable quantity of cattle was captured, and thirty-four Zulus killed, our own loss being small.

The month of February, and the greater part of March, were spent in a similar fashion, constant reconnaissance, and occasional skirmishing. The mere fact that one column was able to keep on persistently harassing the enemy was of great value to Lord Chelmsford, and there is little wonder that he was glad to be able to report even comparatively small successes to the authorities at home. As Sir Garnet Wolseley wrote later to Evelyn Wood:

You and Buller have been the two bright spots in this wretched war.

Another "regrettable incident" occurred on the 12th March. A convoy of supplies on its way to Luneberg was stopped at the Intombi River, which came down in flood when only a portion of the train of wagons had got across the river. The escort was similarly divided, about two-thirds being on the left bank, and the remainder on the right. Early on the morning of the 12th, the camp on the left bank was rushed by Zulus, the officer in command and all but a sixth of his men being *assegaied* on the spot. The party on the right bank made a gallant resistance, under the command of a sergeant, but had to fall back, which it did without loss, and not until it had secured the retreat of several fugitives from the other side of the river. Writing on the 9th March, Buller describes the camp held by the Left Column, and the surrounding country:

We are camping on a spur of the NGaba-ka-Hawana Mountain

PIET UYS

and on very high land about 4,500 feet above the sea. At our back is the NGaba-ka-Hawana, an irregular square with a table top, about 6,400 feet high, and with a very long leg running northward and ending in the Scouterberg or Rough Mountain, under which is the Pivan River. We are on the watershed between the White Umvolosi and the Pemvana, which rising behind us runs northward under the Scouterberg and joins the Pivan; the Umvolosi to the south of us runs practically due east. Due east of us, 14 miles off, rises Mount Zungin, the ground hence to the top being a gradual slope except the last mile, which rises rapidly by stony ridges to a height of nearly 8,000 feet.

Immediately under Zungin and to the south is the Zungin's Neck, on the other side of which is the Inhlobana Mountain, a rocky fastness which is the only place occupied by any force of the Kaffirs within 30 miles of our camp. I have several times asked Colonel Wood to let me attack it, and indeed I did one day attack it without leave, but I had only seventy white men, and had to leave the strongest part of it untouched. There are now about 1,000 Zulus there, and they are getting cheeky. To return to our camp. The cattle *laager* is a circular enclosure made of fifty-two ox-wagons, the pole, or *dissel-boom* as they call it in this country, of one being run under the hind-carriage of the one in front. In the enclosure, which is just 110 yards in diameter, we turn every night our '*trek*' or draught oxen, some 2,000 or 2,600 in number according to circumstances.

There is a nice little sum for Lucy: given a circle of 110 yards in diameter and allowing that 2,200 oxen are put into it, how much ground surface has each ox to lie down upon. Round the circle and inside the outer *laager* are camped the F.L.H., our horses with their heads inwards and the men behind the horses. The outer *laager* is made the same as the inner one of wagons, 135 in number, each wagon occupying about 7 yards of ground. Outside the *laager* are camped the infantry, who on an alarm pull down their tents, and run into the *laager* to defend it. Behind the *laager* is a small fort in which 100 men sleep every night. Thus, we guard ourselves. I do not like this *laager*. The cattle are a great nuisance. We are to move in a couple of days to another site behind the fort as this ground has become foul, and then Wood is going to *laager* on my principle, which will relieve us of the dirt and stink of 2,000 odd oxen.

On the 14th March, Colonel Wood decided on a very bold move. A few days previously a brother of Ketchwayo's, named Uhamu, had come in and given himself up. It was important, from a political point of view, to bring in the wives and families belonging to this chief: Uhamu does not appear to have been quite certain of the strength of his married establishment, but placed it in the neighbourhood of 300 women, besides children. These were in a *kraal* not more than 45 miles from Ulundi, Ketchwayo's capital, in some very rough country between the Black Umvolosi and Mkusi Rivers. The risk was considerable, since if news of the move got to Ulundi there was a good possibility of the rescuing party being cut off on its return march.

Colonel Wood took with him 360 mounted men under Buller and 200 of Uhamu's men, many of whom had fought against the Centre Column at Isandhlwana. The outward march of 45 miles was completed in one day, and without opposition except for some long-range firing from the skirts of the Inhlobana Mountain. The refugees, between 900 and 1,000, of all ages and both sexes, were started off early the next morning, and reached Kambula camp on the 16th, their number having been increased by one child born *en route,* the mother completing the march, unassisted, and arriving in camp before Colonel Wood himself got there.

The night of the 14th, was one of great anxiety. Colonel Wood, a bad sleeper at any time, lay down, but kept waking up throughout the night. Always when he woke he found Buller, who had the valuable soldier's gift of being able to snatch a nap at any odd moment, walking up and down, and round him, to guard him from any disturbance.

The rescued women and children formed a difficult convoy, many of the latter being of very tender years and yet too big to be carried by their mothers. Buller brought up the rear-guard, and though he had stoutly declared that he would have nothing to do with the verminous brats, Wood records having seen him with half a dozen of them in front of and behind his saddle.

As a rule, Zulu children ran away, frightened, from British soldiers (doubtless their mothers used to threaten them when naughty, as English Border children used to be threatened with the Black Douglas), but on this occasion a little girl ran up to Buller with her arms stretched out imploringly for help, and encouraged by her example others followed.

BULLER'S REAR-GUARD ACTION

Writing on the 23rd March, Buller says:

Uhamu's defection will, it is supposed, have a good influence on the events of the war, but I do not myself attach quite so much importance to it as some are inclined to do. He has at least 3,000 fighting men in his portion of the tribe, and of these only about 300 men have come in with the women. Until I see the rest, I shall think that the wily old brute is merely providing for his personal safety on the double event. However, time will show. We had a good deal of trouble getting the women out, as I marched with 300 mounted men about 48 miles into Zululand, camped there and started the next morning with the women.

About half-way back to camp there is a mountain called Inhlobana, which is occupied by about 1,500 Zulus, and I did not want to camp under it, so I forced on the women past it. We certainly made a wonderful march of it, going over 35 miles for us, and as the women had most of them come long distances, over 50 miles for them. Poor things, they were very tired, and during the last two hours begged to be allowed to lie down and die, but we kept them going and got through, only four of the stragglers being *assegaied*, and they were not of the lot I had to guard, but others who had started late and never caught us up. Since I last wrote, the Zulus have caught a detachment of the 80th napping and killed 61 out of 104. It was their fault, but the lesson is an over sharp one.

Again, on the 21st:

I am well but terribly bored at being kept so long in one place. (The papers) are abusing Lord Chelmsford most unmercifully. . . . He has undoubtedly committed serious errors which have culminated in a great disaster, still he is a gentleman and a good fellow, and as he is pleased to think more of my doings up to the present than they merit he will I hope remain out here. I am gradually stepping up the ladder and am now in command of a considerable force of cavalry, having over 560 in camp and 250 more daily expected. I am fearing that the reinforcements from England will bring out so many senior officers that there will be no room for poor junior me, and I shall have to recede to my former position as C.O. of the F.L.H. Still, to have been a Brigadier of Cavalry for even so short a time is something for an infantry captain any way.

My great wish is that they should finish the war and let me get home. If they will only do that quickly I do not care what position they place me in. . . . I have just come back from Luneberg, where I went to hold an inquiry upon the loss of the greater part of a company of the 80th Regiment who were surprised by a force of Zulus in their camp at the Intombi River drift: 61 out of 104 killed, the captain being among the number. It is marvellous to me how men can in the face of an active enemy be so utterly careless. They had a strong position and could have beaten off any amount of Zulus, but took no precautions whatever, and were awoke one morning by finding the enemy inside their camp. It is wonderful how so many escaped. . . .

I am much distressed at the news that has reached me by this mail of the death of Colonel Home, R.E., a friend of mine and a man of great promise, combining ability, energy, and industry in a most unusual degree. His death is a loss to me personally, and besides, or rather beyond, that, it is a loss to the State and to the army. Poor Bob Home, *The Times* may well say that England could have better spared a better-known man. If ever a man worked himself to death for his country that man has.

Home and Buller had served together, as already related, in Ashanti.

The 24th, 25th, and 26th March were taken up with a raid to the Intombi River, where Umbelini, a renegade Swazi, but chief of a Zulu tribe, had been giving a good deal of trouble on the frontier. Two long days were spent in burning the crops of this tribe, and the troops returned to Kambula Hill on the evening of the 26th.

Meanwhile all the necessary preparations had been made by Lord Chelmsford for the relief of Etshowe, and Colonel Wood was requested to make a diversion, with a view to taking pressure off the relieving column. It was decided that this diversion should take the form of an attack on the Zulu stronghold on Inhlobana Mountain, and the following order was issued on the evening of the 26th:

A reconnaissance will be sent to the Inhlobana tomorrow, to be pushed if possible to the top of the mountain on the 28th. The O.C. does not wish Europeans to be engaged in the bush or rocks on either side of the mountain after the summit has been gained. Special precautions will be taken in withdrawing the troops. Lieut.-Colonel Buller, C.B., will make his own arrangements with regard to the hour of starting, taking with him all the mounted men except fifty, who will be left in camp to find the duties.

The 2nd battalion Wood's Irregulars will proceed with Colonel Buller, who will march early tomorrow morning, joining him as he crosses the Zungin Neck. They will bivouac with him, and act under his orders. . . . Lieut.-Colonel Russell (Colonel J. C. Russell, not Baker Russell) will leave camp at 1 p.m. tomorrow, taking with him the M.I., Basutos, 1st battalion Wood's Irregulars and Captain Potter's contingent of Uhamu's men, and will bivouac where the party which brought in Uhamu's people bivouacked, on the way back to camp. . . . Both columns will get as high up the mountain as they conveniently can, on the morning of the 28th, before they can be distinguished.

Lieut.-Colonel Russell's party to ascend the western end of the mountain, advance along the neck, as far as they can without incurring severe loss. It is not intended that the western reconnaissance should force the position against strong resistance, though it will of course advance when it is known that the summit has been gained by the eastern force, or sooner if not strongly opposed.

Major Leet will leave fifty men in camp. As Ketchwayo is said to be advancing with his whole army, Colonel Buller will send scouts to watch the country to the southward, and Colonel Russell scouts towards the Lion's Neck.

Mounted corps will take two days' rations. The remainder three days' rations, groceries and breadstuffs.

Commandant Schermbrucker's corps will join Colonel Russell and act under him.

A rocket tube will accompany each force. The C.R.A. to make the necessary arrangements.—

   (Sd.)   R. Campbell, Captain, S.O.

The strength of the reconnoitring force was as follows: Buller's column, 392 white men, mounted, and 277 natives, and a rocket party; Colonel Russell's, 120 white men, mounted, 510 natives, and a rocket party. The two parties were therefore of about equal strength, but in view of the larger proportion of natives in that commanded by Colonel Russell, Buller's was the stronger fighting force.

Writing on the 30th, he gives the following account of the day's

IRREGULAR MOUNTED CAVALRY OFFICERS SERVING WITH WOOD'S COLUMN

work:

A dispatch had been received from the general saying that he was going to try and relieve Pearson, and that he wished us to make a diversion on the 28th. Wood accordingly decided to try and take the Inhlobana Mountain, a Zulu stronghold, and a most formidable one, about 20 miles to the east of us. I marched, therefore, at 8 on the 27th, with 400 mounted men and some 300 natives and bivouacked on the flats the other side of the Inhlobana, some 30 miles from camp. The programme of the day was that I was to attack and get up the east end of the mountain at all hazards, while Lieut.-Colonel Russell, with about 200 mounted men and 400 natives, was to make a diversion at the west end and get up if he could. Seen in profile the Inhlobana Mountain is much as under.

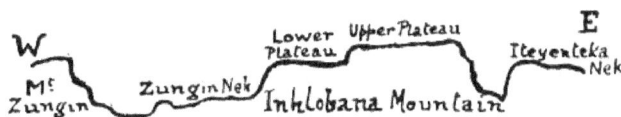

The upper and lower plateaux are each nearly rectangular, the lower one being about 1 mile from east to west, the upper 3 miles from east to west, the lower ½ mile from north to south, the upper 1½ miles. I should say that a portion of my command, consisting of fifty-four volunteers called the Border Horse under a Commandant Weatherley, managed to leave my column on the 27th, and did not rejoin me. Starting at 3 a.m. on the 28th, and favoured by a misty morning, we managed to force our way up the east end of the upper plateau. I think we surprised the Zulus, for Russell was late and gave us no assistance, and the path up was so difficult and so commanded by cross-fire that we could never have got up had the place been properly held. As it was, we only lost two officers killed and one man mortally wounded, all of the F.L.H. to whom I naturally trusted in the brunt of battle. Arrived at the top, I was horrified at the size of the place and its impracticability.

A careful inspection showed me there were only three ways off the top. The one we came by on the east and one at each west corner. Both of the latter were paths such as no man in cold blood would try and get a horse down. I will describe the one at the north-west corner, by which we ultimately descended. This corner was nearly square and the path went down at the angle or rather on the west side of the angle. On each side of the path was a *krantz* (*i.e.* precipice) about 120 feet high. The side precipices were formed of masses of rectangular boulders (if there are such things) piled one over the other in awful confusion, but perpendicularly. At the corner these rocks assumed a certain amount of regularity, and offered a series of insecure footholds or narrow ledges, straight down the precipice and about 8 to 12 feet wide. At the bottom of this path (if path it could be called) was the lower plateau, from which there was another descent of some 800 yards, almost as steep, but less dangerous, as the rocks were filled in with soil, and grass-covered as well.

Colonel Wood gives the following description of this path:

In May, 1880, when on the mountain, I turned the ponies loose and drove them down, allowing them time to pick their way. Nevertheless, one only got down without a fall, and though none were hurt, some rolled for thirty or forty yards on losing their foothold, as, after jumping from the higher crags, they landed on the narrow ledges of rock. ("The Mountain of Valour," *Pearson's Magazine*, 1896.)

Buller got into touch with Russell, somewhere apparently about 8 a.m. The latter had got as far as the lower plateau of Inhlobana at 7. Viewing the path just described from below he decided that it was totally impracticable for horsemen, and consequently made no attempt to take his party by it to the upper plateau.

Being unable to see what was occurring on that part of the mountain, he sent Captain Browne, 24th Foot, with twenty men of the Mounted Infantry to make their way up on foot and communicate with Buller's party. This Browne achieved without meeting opposition, and after speaking to Major Tremlett, R.A., and Major Leet, 1/13th Light Infantry, members of Buller's column, returned with a report that the path was almost impracticable even for men on foot. Buller's narrative continues:

Well, to my tale. Having collected all the cattle we could find, some 2,000, and finding that the Zulus were becoming every minute more in number, and that it was every minute more difficult to prevent them from mustering on the upper plateau,

I proceeded to the east end, sending for my scattered detachments. Arrived there, I sent off Barton, my second in command, down the hill with thirty men. He was to bury Williams and Seitencron, the two officers I had lost, and then he was to return to camp the way we came." (This was by the south side of the mountain: the time was, according to the official history, nearly 9 a.m. To continue:)

Just after we had seen him safe off, we descried a Zulu Army advancing, some 20,000 men in battle (array), across the plain below us. Our position was this, seen from above (see sketch).

We were 30 miles from camp: our horses had been under saddle since 3 a.m., it was then 10, and they had had nothing to eat really since the previous morning.

I saw that we had not a chance of getting back the way we came, so I at once sent two men after Barton, telling him to return by the right of the mountain. Alas, for the use of careless words! By 'right' I meant the north side. Poor Barton, going down the mountain with his back to it (facing east), understood that he was to turn to *his* right, and so went to the left, or south side, on which was the Zulu *impi*.

★★★★★★

Note:—At the same time, a man going west, and told to go "by the right of the mountain," would, it might be expected, keep to the north side, with the mountain on his left. But as it seems to have been a verbal order, it may have miscarried in the telling.

★★★★★★

To attack them he called up Colonel Weatherley with the Border Horse, whom he saw on the plain below. They could not get through, but lost many men in the attempt. They then turned and attempted to get back by the path on the north side of the mountain. They were pursued in force. Poor dear Barton and half his men were killed, and Colonel Weatherley and forty-four of his Border Horse were killed also. Barton had been my constant companion since he joined me in July. We lived in the one tent, every day I saw something to like him more for, and he is a dreadful loss. I am still hoping against hope, as no one actually saw him killed, that he may turn up. One of Weatherley's men came in yesterday, having been two days hidden in long grass.

ZULUS ATTACKING

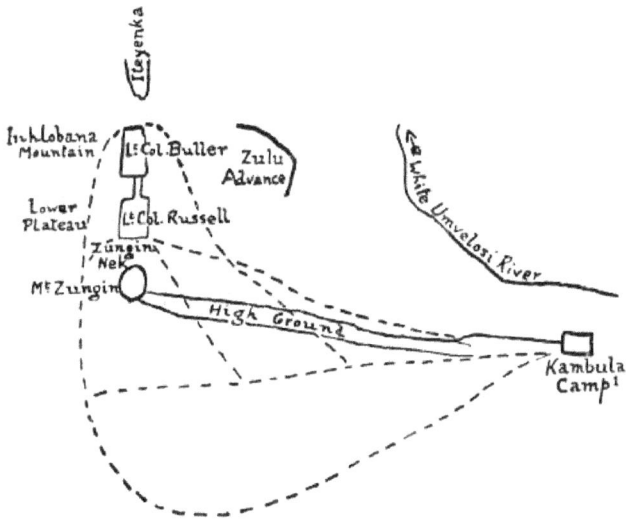

DOTTED LINES SHOW TRACKS BETWEEN KAMBULA AND INHLOBANA.

Colonel Russell saw the approaching Zulu Army almost at the same time as Colonel Buller saw it. He immediately sent off a report of the fact to Colonel Wood, whom he believed to be on the upper plateau. Colonel Wood had followed on Buller's tracks, picking up on his way Colonel Weatherley and the Border Horse who had lost touch with Buller's column during the night. He ordered them to march to the sound of the firing now audible on the north-east face of the mountain, where the tail of Buller's column could be seen mounting the summit. Pushing on ahead with his staff, he became engaged with Zulus hiding amongst caves and rock-shelters of the mountain-side.

Two of his staff, Captain Hon. R. Campbell and Mr. Lloyd, his political assistant, were killed almost at once, and after recovering the bodies he went some distance down the hill to bury them. Whilst thus engaged he was fired at by a body of Zulus, about 600 strong, who were advancing from the direction of the Ityenteka Nek. These he was able to hold in check with the assistance of some of Buller's men who had not yet rejoined their commander. By the time he had finished this operation it was about 10 o'clock, and all was quiet on the upper plateau. He decided, therefore, to search for Russell's column, and see how they had fared.

Whilst moving slowly along the foot of the south wall of Inhlobana he became aware of the approach of the Zulu *impi* on his left flank, and at once (10.30 a.m.) sent off his orderly officer (Lieut. H. Lysons,

63

190th Foot—awarded V.C) with a warning message to Colonel Russell, ending, "Get into position on the Zungin Nek." This crossed the message already sent off by Colonel Russell, an hour and a half earlier, which Colonel Wood, apparently, never received: it was seen, however, by Colonel Buller at 9.20.

Meanwhile the *impi* had advanced rapidly, and at 10 o'clock Colonel Russell ordered his men to abandon the cattle they had collected, and to retire to the plain below the west end of the mountain. Arrived there he dispatched his native troops to Kambula Camp, and with the remainder made arrangements to cover the retirement of Buller's people from the lower plateau. He received Colonel Wood's message at 10.45, and unaware that his own message had not reached that officer, he at once withdrew, according to orders, to Zungin Nek. Unfortunately, there was some doubt as to the actual place intended, and whilst he moved to the point where the track from Kambula crosses the western end of the Zungin Mountain, Colonel Wood waited for him at the eastern end of the same range, there being a distance of 6 miles between the two places. It is now time to return to Colonel Buller's movements; his narrative proceeds:

> To return to my own fortunes. With the bulk of my men I decided to descend on to the lower plateau by the path I have described, where I supposed Russell was, and whence we could get back to camp easily by the east of Zungin, if we could avoid the Zulu Army, and fairly easily by the north and west if we could not. But on reaching the top of the path (official history gives the time as 10 a.m.) I found Russell had gone and my retreat was uncovered. We had to get down the frightful path under a constant and ever-increasing fire, but we should have done so tolerably safely I believe had not my stupid rear-guard ceased firing, mistaking Zulus for friends.
>
> In a moment the Zulus were among us in the rocks. How I got down I shall never know. Here we lost one officer and sixteen men, and Mr. Piet Uys, whose name you must have often seen in the papers since the war began to attract interest at home. He was my guide, counsellor, and friend. His loss is a most serious one to all South Africa and irreparable to me. He really was the finest man, morally speaking, that I ever met.
>
> When I got to the bottom there was sort of panic: most of the men were dismounted, and for a moment I feared a catastro-

Running Zulu Impi

phe, but they soon rallied, and we got down the mountain and home without much further loss, though as the enemy followed, firing for some miles, we lost a few by bullet wounds. We got back to camp rather downhearted, as you may imagine, but of my column of 404 Europeans, ten officers and eighty men failed to answer to their names, and eleven more were wounded. To add to our grief, when I returned to camp, I found that Colonel Wood had tried to follow me up the path I assaulted in the morning, and that Campbell and Lloyd were killed, so our losses were altogether very heavy to say nothing of the natives. Poor 'Rowdy' Campbell, he was such a good fellow. It was a bad day; I hope I shall never see such another.

As usual when writing about himself Buller tends to baldness in his narration. Fortunately, Sir Evelyn Wood has left two excellent accounts of the retirement down the west end of Inhlobana (*From Midshipman to Field-Marshal* and *The Mount of Valour, Pearson's Magazine*, 1896): there is also the official history, from which it is possible to fill in the essential detail.

When Buller first saw the approaching Zulu *impi* it was about 6 miles from Inhlobana: he calculated that this would give him about an hour before he could be seriously harassed by the advanced parties of this body. About 2.000 cattle had been collected, but these had been sent down at 7 o'clock, and driven off in the direction of the Zungin Nek

It was about 10 o'clock when the retreat began. The native troops went first, and then the mounted men in succession, the Frontier Light Horse staying to the last. Even if the descent had been unmolested the task of getting tired horses down that difficult path would have been sufficiently difficult.

Unfortunately, the Amaqulisi, who formed the garrison of Inhlobana, had also seen the advance of the Zulu *impi* and began to collect in great numbers, assailing, not only the rear-guard holding the head of the path, but also the straggling line of dismounted troopers who were making their way down. Clambering along the sides of the mountain they fired into these men at close range, even occasionally attacking hand-to-hand with their *assegais*. Major Leet of the 13th Light Infantry, in spite of an injury to his knee which disabled him from walking, had stayed with Buller till ordered to retire. He, with Lieut. Smith and a trooper of the Frontier Light Horse, got separated from the main stream of men, and were attacked by Zulus when half-way down. The trooper was stabbed; Smith, who had sat down exhausted, would have met a similar fate had not Major Leet, double banking his horse, carried him into safety. For this gallant deed Major Leet received the Victoria Cross.

At length only seven men of the Frontier Light Horse were left at the top with Lieut. Everitt and Colonel Buller. As soon as they turned to descend, four of the troopers were killed, and Everitt's horse was stabbed. Buller dragged Everitt out of the way of the enemy and ordered him down; then seizing his carbine and ammunition he joined the three surviving troopers in covering his retreat.

Mr. Piet Uys, who had been sent down some time before to get together a party on the lower plateau, to cover the descent of the rearguard, seeing his youngest son in difficulties returned to help him, and was killed, just as Everitt arrived at the foot of the descent. The men were now thoroughly demoralised, but Buller, with the aid of some of their officers, managed to restore a certain amount of order. The wounded and those who had lost their horses were put up behind the mounted men, and eventually the survivors were collected at the foot of the mountain.

Buller seems to have led a charmed life. All through the day, whether fighting with the rearguard on the edge of the cliff, or clambering down the "Devil's Staircase" that led to the lower plateau, or the only less difficult descent to the plain, he was always present where the need was greatest. Amidst all the confusion and uproar of the retreat, he, almost alone, remained calm and self-possessed, steadying the panic-stricken men by an occasional quiet reassuring remark, "All will go well," or, "We are all going to get down safely," so that, as one of them said afterwards, they felt confident and safe, even in the midst of extreme danger.

It was due to his exertions and desperate courage, and even more to his commanding personality, that the retreat did not turn into a rout and a massacre.

He personally saved four men's lives. One man, who was killed later in the day, he dragged out from a struggling crowd of Zulus, and carried for the time being into safety; returning, he picked up another from in front of the rapidly advancing enemy, and did him the same service. Again, he went back, and brought in Captain D'Arcy, of the Frontier Light Horse, who, having lost both his horses, was panting along on foot, tired out, and with little hope of distancing his pursuers. Lieut. Everitt was the fourth. But indeed, it is not too much to say that every wounded or dismounted man of his party who got back to camp that evening owed his life to the skill and courage with which Buller handled his command.

Even when he had returned to camp his work was not finished. At 9 o'clock a solitary horseman came in and reported that half a dozen stragglers were still out on the *veldt*, trying to find their way to Kambula. Buller at once collected a dozen volunteers, and riding out into the pitch-black night brought in these last survivors of the day.

> Buller and his men had been almost continuously in the saddle for one hundred consecutive hours, during which time they had skirmished once, fought twice, and marched over 170 miles.

There can be fewer finer records of leadership, courage, and endurance than that of the Frontier Light Horse and their commander during those four days.

They had no long rest. In the letter already quoted, Buller continues:

> On the 29th, as we were sadly musing over the events of the day before, our scouts came in to say that the Zulu Army we had left in the valley below were on the move, and about 10 they came in sight, moving in five very heavy columns. We at once commenced preparations for defence. Our *laager* now is thus:

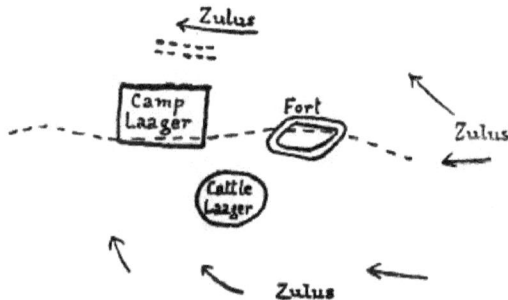

The fort on high ground commands both cattle *laager* and camp, but owing to the nature of the ground the position is on a ridge with narrow top and steep sides. The dotted line shows the crest line, consequently the cattle *laager* is not well commanded by the camp. We set all straight and waited for the fray. As they got nearer, I went out with the mounted men and attacked the head of the right column. They stood our advance for a little, the dots (in the sketch) being my men, and if anything, they edged off somewhat to their right in order to pursue their flanking movement. But they could not stand our attack as I pressed home, and the advance of their right column, about 2,000 strong, turned and charged us. I need not say that the eighty or ninety men I had got on their horses pretty quick, and we scampered back to camp holding a running fight with them as we went. Our attack succeeded. It was evident it upset their plans, for during the whole day that corner of the camp remained unsurrounded. In a very short time, the attack began in earnest and the position always was thus:

the dark lines being Zulus and A, B, C our entrenchments. They did not have quite enough discipline to fill up the gaps caused to their admirably laid plans. The attack continued for about four hours, the Zulus developing all their strength, about 22,000: we being about 2,100 all told. Our position, which was a very strong one to defend, was a bad one from which to inflict loss upon the enemy, as the hill we are camped on slopes so much we cannot see its foot, and there they collected for their rushes. We suffered considerably. I don't know how much, but I should say at least seventy killed and wounded, principally by Martini-Henry bullets, that had, I suppose, been captured at Isandlana.

At 4.30 p.m., it was: 'Stand to your horses, mounted men.' We were up and at them. Had it not been dark their loss would have been very heavy. Still, I cannot think that the killed and wounded in the pursuit was less than 300 at the least. So ended my two days' fighting in Zululand. I pray you may not have heard I was killed on the 28th. Some wicked man so reported, and it may just have got down and caught a mail before the contradiction. Please do not be over-anxious about me. Ill news flies apace, but do not believe I am hurt till you see it officially.

There is hardly need to add much to Buller's account of Kambula.

The skill with which he handled his mounted men in the earliest phase of the engagement had the effect of disorganising the Zulu scheme of attack, and their right column did but little during the rest of the day. Their left and centre, however, pressed on with great gallantry, and even captured the cattle *kraal*, which Buller mentions as not being well commanded from the camp. They collected in large numbers behind the ridge, preparatory to rushing the main position, but a gallant charge by two companies of the 90th Foot, under Major Hackett, who was very severely wounded, checked their onslaught.

The artillery also distinguished themselves, fighting their guns in the open. The British loss was eighteen N.C.O.'s and men killed, and 65 of all ranks wounded. Ten of the latter died of their wounds, a very high percentage. The Zulu losses were out of all proportion, amounting to about 2,000. The army that was engaged on this occasion dispersed after the battle, and the district remained quiet during the rest of the campaign.

He writes again on the 5th of April:

I have been having to work double tides lately, having no one to replace either poor dear affectionate little Bobby Barton, my second in command, or Alan Gardner, my staff officer (wounded). . . . You will see an account of our fighting in the *Standard*, as a correspondent for that paper turned up here two days ago, after the battle. The rascal tried three times to interview me, but I knew too much for him, and he had to send off his report without even so much as getting a question into me. . . . Poor 'Rowdy' Campbell, Rachel Howard's brother, is a great loss, not only as a pleasant, cheery, bright companion, but as an officer. He was an excellent one, and I regret to say that good Staff officers are scarce articles in these parts just now.

I was very much pleased with the Frontier Light Horse on the 28th, under most difficult circumstances; they really did well, and those of them that we could get hold of rallied quickly. It was a bad quarter of an hour though, and when next I have a turn at the Hlobana Mountain I trust it may be under more favourable circumstances. As for the Zulu War, I begin to fear that it will never be over. I hope that in ten days' time we shall be able to move forward. I fancy our halting place will be somewhere near the east end of Mt. Ingwe: you will see it on the map near the White Umvolosi River. If we can build a good fort there and fill it up with supplies, we then go to the Inhlazatye Mountain, the most difficult part of the whole road, by the way, and from thence I with the mounted men ought to be able to burn Ulundi.

The letter just quoted is interesting for two reasons. It illustrates in the first place his deeply affectionate nature. This was a trait that, being intensely shy and reserved, he kept carefully concealed. He did not "carry his heart on his sleeve for daws to peck at," and those who knew him superficially did not give him credit for the depth of his feelings. In addition, it gives an instance of his obsession in the matter of war correspondents. As a class, he distrusted them, and in this campaign at least, one correspondent gave him good reason for this feeling. This gentleman, I quote from Colonel Lewis Butler:

> Who had been treated with confidence, actually told Colonel Buller that he considered himself justified in reading and making use of any private correspondence he might happen to find, and was surprised next day to be turned out of the colonel's tent.

A man capable of holding such opinions is hardly likely to inspire trust in his hearer. But mainly Buller's dislike of correspondents was due to his hatred of anything that savoured of self-advertisement. He carried the feeling to excess, no doubt, but at least there was nothing sordid about it. One can hardly say the same of the conduct of some men who have erred in the opposite direction. Still, it may be conceded that it was a mistake, and it certainly did him no good.

For his gallantry during the fighting on Inhlobana, Buller was recommended for the Victoria Cross by Evelyn Wood, who gives the following account of the matter (*From Midshipman to Field-Marshal*):

> I had heard many stories of the gallantry shown by Colonel Buller in the retreat from the western end of the Inhlobana, but I had some difficulty in arriving at anything definite, because he guarded closely all the mounted men from receiving orders except through him, and I knew from his character that he would repudiate the notion of having done anything more than his duty. A few days after the fight he went out ... to endeavour to find Captain Barton's body. While he was out, I received written statements from Lieutenants D'Arcy and Everitt and Trooper Rundall, whom he had rescued at the risk of his life, and their reports were verified by those of other officers who

HOW HE WON THE VICTORIA CROSS.
GENERAL BULLER.

were present. This enabled me to put forward a strong recommendation that his name should be considered for the Victoria Cross. A day or two later ... I said ... I think you may be interested in something I have written and I handed him the letter-book. He was very tired (after an unsuccessful raid) and observed somewhat ungraciously, 'Some nonsense, I suppose,' to which I replied, 'Yes, I think I have been rather eulogistic' When he handed me back the book his face was a study.

Buller's reckless bravery gave his commander many anxious moments. His staff officer, Captain Campbell, wrote that whenever the former went out on a raid Wood was unable to keep quiet, but was restless from sheer anxiety till his return to camp. Later in England, Wood told Buller's sister that he had earned the V.C. every time he went out in Zululand.

He would never, however great the personal risk, leave a wounded man behind, whose rescue was compatible with the performance of the duty on which he was engaged.

The Battle of Kambula and the relief of Etshowe mark the end of the second phase of the Zulu War. Reinforcements were now arriving, and by the middle of April all those dispatched from England had landed in Natal. The force at Lord Chelmsford's disposal was now rearranged in two divisions, a Cavalry Brigade and a Flying Column.

The 1st Division (six battalions, three batteries, etc.), under the command of Major-General H. H. Crealock, was ordered to advance on much the same line as that taken by the original 1st Column.

The 2nd Division (four battalions, two batteries, etc.), under Major-General Newdigate, and the Cavalry Brigade (two regiments), under Major-General Marshall, advanced in an easterly direction from the neighbourhood of Utrecht. Lord Chelmsford accompanied this force.

The Flying Column, commanded by Brig.-General Evelyn Wood, V.C., was practically the original 4th Column, reinforced by the addition of one battalion and a battery. It was, in addition, much strengthened in the mounted arm, which was now increased to 1,400 Irregular Horse, under Lieut. Colonel Buller. He had beyond all cavil earned the right to this advancement, nevertheless it was an undoubted stroke of luck for an infantry officer, who in his own regiment ranked as a captain, to get the command of what in point of numbers was equivalent to a Cavalry Brigade.

After the Battle of Kambula the troops commanded by General

Wood had a period of comparative rest. The time was taken up in organising the transport and collecting supplies at Utrecht and Balte Spruit, in preparation for the final advance. The country was quiet and convoys between those two places and Kambula were not interfered with.

A correspondent, writing from Kambula on the 15th of April, gives a picture of Buller at this period. He wore

> What has been a large broad-brimmed soft felt hat of light colour, wrapped round with a distinguishing *puggaree* of red cloth, a coloured flannel shirt, nothing round his neck, a tweed shooting jacket, cord breeches cased with leather round the knees, brown-leather butcher boots, and spurs, and a revolver, bestriding a stout pony of fourteen hands that looks barely up to his weight. The clothing of his men followed no exact rule, but the most usual was a cord jacket, trousers of a peculiar olive-brown tint, high-low boots, and gaiters. Round the soft felt hat was worn a distinguishing *puggaree*, that of the Frontier Light Horse being red, the same as worn by their commander.
>
> For armament Buller preferred a carbine, with the ammunition carried *en bandolier*. Sabres he would not be troubled with, saying that he was sure that if his men had been so armed on Inhlobana, they would never have got up the hill, and if they had would most certainly not have come off it alive. Those who could obtain them carried a groundsheet and waterproof cloak, or in winter a blanket and greatcoat. Those who were unable to procure these articles went without them, and campaigned in what they stood up in, with the addition of a quart pot and a jack-knife.

We have another portrait of him, at about the same time, describing his appearance whilst in action. During a reconnaissance the Zulus had allowed the main body of the party to pass on, with the intention of attacking them from behind. Evelyn Wood detecting the ruse ordered twenty men to wheel about and charge the enemy gathering in his rear. Buller headed the charge:

> Leading his men at a swinging canter, with his reins in his teeth, a revolver in one hand, and a *knobkerrie* he had snatched from a Zulu in the other, his hat blown off in the *mêlée*, and a large streak of blood across his face, caused by a splinter of rock from above, this gallant horseman seemed a demon incarnate to the

flying savages, who slunk out of his path as if he had been—as indeed they believed him—an evil spirit, whose very look was death.

The month of May was spent in reconnoitring with a view to deciding on the best line of advance into the enemy's country. There were several of these expeditions, none furnishing any striking incident, but in the aggregate representing a great deal of hard work, and supplying useful, in fact indispensable, information. In one of them, carried out between the 14th and 16th days of the month, Buller was accompanied by the Prince Imperial, who distinguished himself by his disregard of danger. On the 29th the Flying Column was completed up to strength by the arrival of five companies of the 80th Foot, and a battery of four gatlings.

The main advance began on the 1st June, the plan being that the Flying Column should always be about half a march in front of the main body of the 2nd Division. On the day in question, the Flying Column having arrived at its camp ground on the right bank of the Umyamyene River, Wood and Buller rode out to examine the country in front. Sir George Pomeroy Colley gives the following account of what happened:

> Evelyn Wood and Buller were riding ahead of the column as usual to look out for a good camping ground, when suddenly they saw an officer riding furiously towards them—so furiously that Buller observed, 'Why, the man rides as if he thought the Kaffirs were after him.' As he came nearer, he gesticulated wildly and beckoned them to go back, but they rode on till they met him. 'Whatever is the matter with you?' said Buller. 'The prince—the Prince Imperial is killed,' was all the man could gasp out, breathless and wild. 'Where—where is the body?' asked Buller sharply. The man could only gasp and point to a hill about 3 miles off, from which they could now see some twenty Kaffirs going away in the opposite direction with three led horses.
>
> 'Where are your men, sir? How many did you lose?' said Buller sharply and sternly, now thoroughly roused. 'They are behind me—I don't know,' stammered the unfortunate man. Then said Buller, turning on him savagely, 'You deserve to be shot, and I hope will be. I could shoot you myself,' and turned his back on him. Had it been either Wood or Buller, they would have

turned had it been a thousand Kaffirs, and probably would have brought him away.

On which the only comment that occurs to one is that neither Wood nor Buller would have allowed themselves to get trapped in the way that these unfortunate men were trapped, through sheer carelessness. Fierce as his resentment at this unhappy officer's conduct was in the shock of the first news of the tragedy, his sense of justice led him later to urge in extenuation the fact that it was the man's first time under fire, and that another time he might do better. To the end of his career he refused to condemn a man for one mistake, withstanding even the orders of government if necessary, in the accused's defence.

The advance continued throughout the month of June, the Flying Column leading the way until at the close of the month the force was within a short distance of Ulundi, Ketchwayo's capital. On the 3rd July, Buller was sent forward with the mounted men of the Flying Column to select a good position for the force to take up if attacked on its advance to Ulundi. Lord Chelmsford also wished to force the enemy to show his numbers and plan of attack. Buller manoeuvred his men with great skill. Whilst he was engaged with a strong body of the enemy in his front, large masses gathered on his flanks and tried to encircle him.

He retired his force in alternate parties, each in turn covering the retirement of the other, and, having obtained for Lord Chelmsford the information he desired, returned to camp with the loss of three men killed and four wounded. It was in this skirmish that Lord William Beresford, who had been acting as Staff officer to Buller since the column left Kambula, earned the Victoria Cross. Captain D'Arcy also distinguished himself by picking up a wounded man from close to the advancing enemy. Lord Chelmsford afterwards attributed much of his success in the final battle to Buller's management of this reconnaissance.

The next day, the 4th July, the whole force advanced, the mounted men of the Flying Column, under Buller, as usual, leading the way. After crossing the Umvolosi the main body advanced through rough scrub jungle until it reached the open country beyond. Here it was formed into a hollow rectangle, the sides of which were about twice the length of the front and rear faces. In this formation, with Buller's men covering the advance, and the cavalry guarding the flanks and rear the force marched till it came within a mile and a half of Ulundi, to the spot selected by Buller the day before.

It was now about half-past eight, and at about a quarter to nine the mounted men on the front and right flank came into action against the enemy, who had begun to assemble on the surrounding heights, soon after the column emerged from the bushy ground. The horsemen were gradually driven back and took refuge inside the rectangle. The Zulus attacked on all sides, but showed neither the resolution nor the tactical skill they had exhibited at Kambula. They were unable to stand up against the artillery and rifle fire, and at 9.25 a.m., the 17th Lancers were let loose from the rear face of the square in pursuit. Buller led his men out from the front face soon afterwards, and joined in dispersing various scattered bodies of the enemy now in full flight.

Evelyn Wood, in his dispatch on this day's doings says:

Colonel Buller gave us such aid as has seldom been afforded by light cavalry to a main body of troops.

This is particularly in reference to his action on the 3rd and 4th July, but it is equally true of his work during the whole of the advance of the 2nd Division.

The Battle of Ulundi marked the end of the Zulu War. The Zulus never collected again; Ketchwayo became a fugitive, and was eventually captured on the 20th August.

There are unfortunately no letters of Buller's extant for the period between the Battles of Kambula and Ulundi.

He writes on the 10th July, nearly a week after the latter:

Times are hard and paper and grub both short, so I must use up an old bit to write to you. . . . I have sent in a medical certificate, so I hope to get away in about thirty days from now, but possibly I may not get out quite so soon, for there are one or two things that I have to do that may take me some little time. Among others, I want to get hold of poor old Piet Uys' bones and bury them, also Barton's, if I can. All this in this big country may take time, but I trust that I shall be off at the time I say. I was much amused at the concluding paragraph of your letter, telling me to be civil to correspondents, as the day before I received it, I had had to pull one through a thorn bush to teach him manners. He was the special of the ———; please, if he revenges himself in caricaturing me, buy a copy and keep it for me.

As far as I can see, fighting is over, for we gave the Zulus such a dressing on the 4th that, fine fellows as they are, they can never come to time again to attack us. ... We have burned and left Ulundi. Newdigate's division is marching down to bring up supplies, and we are moving across country through Kwamagasa to St. Paul's mission station, where we are to help General Crealock's column up in its march from the mouth of the Umlatosi River (Port Durnford) through Ondine towards us. Between the mouth of the Umlatosi and St. Paul's there is a good deal of thick bush. I am so looking forward to going home that I can hardly write about anything else. If I do get home, we shall be a pleasant party. E. Wood, Bill Beresford, Teddy Prior, self, and some other congenial spirits; we shall be able to fight our battles o'er and o'er again all the way home. Some of them I have no wish to fight again in any other way.

Sir Garnet Wolseley, who had come out to take supreme Civil and Military charge at the Cape, was very anxious to keep both Wood and Buller with him, to assist him in settling Sekukuni's business. They were, however, both so completely run down by the fatigues and exposure of the last sixteen months that longer stay in the field was out of the question. Buller suffered from an obstinate unhealed wound, and his legs and hands were covered with *veldt* sores. Wolseley had perforce to let them go, but he published a very handsome farewell order, recording:

His high appreciation of the services they have rendered during the war, which their military ability and untiring energy have so largely contributed in bringing to an end. The success which has attended the operations of the Flying Column is largely due to General Wood's genius for war, to the admirable system he established in his command, and to the zeal and energy with which his ably conceived plans have been carried out by Colonel Buller.

Lord Chelmsford gave them equally high praise, calling them, in a speech made by him at Pietermaritzburg, "my right and left supporters during the whole of my time in the country."

It may be mentioned here that Piet Uys' body was recovered, but the remains of Captain Barton were not found till May of the next year, when Sir Evelyn Wood, who was in the suite of Her Imperial Majesty the Empress Eugenie, had a search made for them. The incidents of Barton's death and the finding of his body are related in Sir Evelyn's book, *From Midshipman to Field-Marshal*.

Statements made in farewell orders are like those on memorial tablets, "not on oath," but Sir Garnet's letter to the commander-in-chief was equally complimentary (18.7.79):

The men who have been the life and soul of this war are Brigadier-General Wood and Lieutenant-Colonel Buller. If their advice had been steadily acted upon, I believe that no further operations would have been necessary now. . . . I am extremely sorry that I have been obliged to allow both Brigadier-General Wood and Lieutenant-Colonel Buller to return home. Both are pretty well worn out, and both require rest for mind as well as for body. I feel their loss beyond measure, as I had looked to them to finish this business, and then to wind up matters for me in the Transvaal when I go there.

Some newspaper started the report that Buller and Wood left South Africa because they did not agree with Sir Garnet Wolseley's policy with regard to the Transvaal. As a matter of fact, they were both very seriously run down. In the case of Buller, this dated back to the time of Kambula. When the force collected before the move on Ulundi, Lord Chelmsford asked Evelyn Wood, "What have you been doing with Buller?"

"Working him to death and giving him nothing to eat," was the reply. Redvers Buller never quite got over the effects of the campaign. Up to that time he had been a spare though large-framed man; from this date onwards, he inclined to become heavy, whilst his hands were so crippled with *veldt* sores that his handwriting was permanently affected.

Buller sailed from Cape Town in the S.S. *German* on the 5th of August, arriving at Plymouth on the 26th of the same month. On his way to London he was met and greeted at Exeter by the vicar and some of the parishioners of St. Thomas', Exeter, of which he was Lord of the Manor. The chief welcome from his fellow-townsmen was, however, a week later when he returned to Downes. A *feu de joie* of fog-signals at Crediton station, flags and mottoes of welcome along the road, and a cheering crowd who dragged his carriage to his own door, signified the affection and pride with which his own people welcomed his return to them.

A month later, not only his town, but the whole county of Devon did him honour at a great banquet in the Victoria Hall, Exeter. Dinners unfortunately involve speech-making, and to Buller, having to listen to his own praises, was only less painful an ordeal than having to reply to them. He made no pretence to oratory, but what he did say was characterised by his innate straightforwardness and common sense.

Soon after his return to England he was commanded to Balmoral, where he was received by the queen. A recent writer has described Buller as "unintelligent." That certainly was not the impression received of him by that unequalled judge of character, Queen Victoria. The following letter was written by Lady Ely, one of Her Majesty's Ladies-in-Waiting, to his aunt, Lady Suffolk, after this visit:

> The queen desires me to tell you how much pleased Her Majesty is with Colonel Buller, who has been here with Sir Evelyn Wood, and only left this morning. Her Majesty found him so clever and intelligent and so modest about himself. The queen liked his manner so much. Her Majesty feels sure you will like to know how much he has been liked and appreciated.

It is said that the court in general were rather startled at the frankness of his conversation with the queen, to which he replied:

> If I am not to tell the truth to my sovereign, I don't know to whom I am to tell it.

A few days after his Balmoral visit, he received an invitation to Hughenden, from Lord Beaconsfield, in the following terms:

> The queen wishes me to see you, but it is not merely in obedience to Her Majesty's commands, but for my own honour and gratification that I venture to say that if your engagements permit I should be happy to see you here on the 25th inst.

There could hardly have been a greater compliment to a rising soldier than this invitation from the most prominent statesman in Europe. Buller, however, declined it, not because as a traditional Whig he disapproved of Lord Beaconsfield's politics (in fact, on Imperial questions he very much agreed with the Premier's line of action), but because the latter had refused, even at the Royal command, to receive a visit from Lord Chelmsford. Buller was fond of his late commander, though he thought by no means highly of some of his work in Zululand, and his innate loyalty made it impossible for him to share in what might look like a slur on his chief.

The fifteen months spent in South Africa had been very fruitful to Buller, both in honour and substantial reward. He went out a comparatively unknown Captain of Infantry, with a Brevet Majority and a C.B. He returned with a C.M.G. (bestowed for his services in the Amatola Mountains) and with a well-earned decoration for personal courage. In addition, he was made an A.D.C. to the queen, which appointment carried with it the rank of colonel in the army: the prize which he had thought hardly within his reach a few months earlier.

Professionally he stood out as one of the first fighting soldiers in the army. Though all his previous training had been that of Light Infantry, he showed that he possessed all the qualities of a born leader of Partisan Horse, such a one as Stuart or Ashby of the Confederate Army, while at the same time he was free from the besetting sin of such leaders: the tendency to play each for his own hand.

His later career was to show that he possessed another quality not usually found in men of this stamp, and generally considered incompatible with the character, the power of business-like attention to the details of office administration.

But most important of all, his command of the Frontier Light Horse gave him his first opportunity of exhibiting his wonderful power of winning the personal affection of the men who served under him. This power he retained to the end of his career. In spite of the fact that for nearly twelve years he had been in the War Office, cut off from all contact with the daily life of the soldier, and in spite of the fact that high rank and great responsibility made the close personal relationship with the rank and file, which was possible in 1879, for the Commander of the Frontier Light Horse, no longer feasible for the Commander-in-Chief of the Natal Army twenty years later, nevertheless he won from the men who served under him in 1899, the same love and respect that had been paid him by the men of his regiment in Zululand. And in the one case as in the other this love came unsought, as the reward of a selfless and unheralded devotion to the interests of his men.

Sir Redvers H. Buller, V.C and the
Ashanti and Zulu Wars

Contents

CHAPTER 1

The Ashanti War

In 1873 Captain Buller was transferred from his regiment, then still stationed in British North America, to the Staff College, and before the year was out, he was again selected for active duty. Having served in Asia and in North America, he was now destined to serve in the Dark Continent, with different parts of which his later achievements on active service were destined to be connected. The new war which was to give him fresh employment was one against King Coffee, an Ashanti chieftain who had imprisoned European missionaries, attacked the less warlike Fantis, England's allies, on the West Coast of Africa, and even claimed Elmina, the next settlement to Cape Coast Castle, and invaded the Gold Coast territory.

There had been petty warfare going on for ten years when the British Government resolved to put a stop to it by sending out an Expedition which, while making use of native troops, should suffice to awe King Coffee into submission and bring about a peace. It was decided that:

> England could not allow the territories of the tribes in allegiance with Her Majesty to be devastated, the inhabitants butchered or driven away into slavery, and all progress and commerce stopped on the coast by hordes of barbarians.

General Wolseley, who had so distinguished himself in the Red River Expedition, was appointed to the command of the forces to be employed against the Ashantis, and was at the same time appointed governor of the country; and around him, as we shall see, rallied many officers who had served with him in Canada, among them being Captain Redvers Buller.

The terms on which General Wolseley was empowered to make

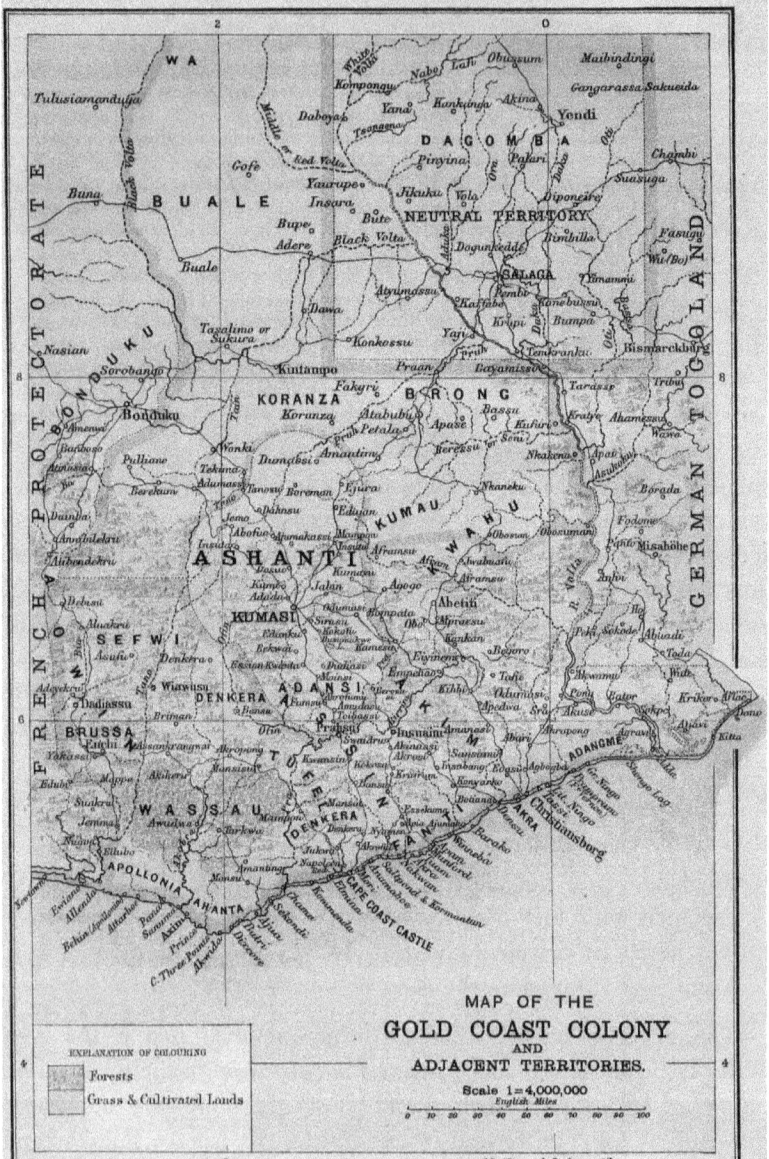

MAP OF THE

GOLD COAST COLONY
AND
ADJACENT TERRITORIES.

Scale 1=4,000,000

English Miles

0 10 20 30 40 50 60 70 80 90 100

WA

DAGOMBA

NEUTRAL TERRITORY

BUALE

BONDUKU

KORANZA BRONG

KUMAU

ASHANTI

KWAHU

KUMASI

SEFWI

DENKERA ADANSI

BRUSSA

WASSAU

DENKERA

APOLLONIA AHANTA

CAPE COAST CASTLE

FRENCH PROTECTORATE

GERMAN TOGOLAND

SALAGA

Yendi

Bismarckburg

Kumasi

Meridian of 0 Greenwich.

The Edinburgh Geographical Institute

J.G.Bartholomew.

peace are well summarised from the official instructions by the historian of this war:—

A lasting peace is required—and a peace on conditions such as these:

A renewed renunciation of the king's rights over the Protectorate and Elmina.

The keeping open of paths in Ashanti and promotion of commerce through the interior with the coast.

The safe release of the European missionaries.

The release of all prisoners taken from the protected tribes.

Hostages of distinction given to us.

An indemnity for the war expenses, and for the injuries inflicted on our allies.

If possible, the diminution or cessation of human sacrifices and slave-hunting on the part of the Ashantis.

Such terms of peace as these could evidently not be hoped for from an enemy in actual possession of the territory he claimed, stopping all passage to the interior, holding captive not only the European missionaries but hundreds of slaves taken from the Protectorate, living on the produce of the land he had invaded, and sacrificing Fanti slaves on the death of every chief, unless by giving him an idea of our power to enforce our demands, vastly different from that he must derive by seeing us hemmed in and confined to a narrow strip of seaboard by his victorious troops.

Such were the terms on which General Wolseley was to make peace with King Coffee and his warriors, but he was at the same time given very strongly to understand that, owing to the notoriously bad climate (the Gold Coast is commonly known as "the white man's grave"), he was to be very chary of having recourse to warfare rendering necessary the employment of a large force of British officers and soldiers. The gloomiest forebodings were indulged in in England when the Expedition was arranged; but despite all those forebodings, and despite the deadly nature of the Gold Coast climate, many officers volunteered for service with the young general, who must have been especially pleased at the ready way in which the men who had been on his Staff during the Red River Expedition offered to enlist under him on his new and unpromising command.

GUARDING ZULU PRISONERS

When Wolseley set sail from Liverpool in the steamer *Ambriz*, on September 12, 1873, it must have been particularly gratifying to him to find around him as members of his Staff no fewer than five of his old comrades. Of these the one that here especially interests us is Captain Redvers Buller, to whom was allotted the part of Deputy-Assistant-Quartermaster-General. That this little band of officers consisted of men little likely to be easily discouraged might have been imagined, both from what they had gone through in their efforts to put down the Louis Riel rising, and also from the very fact of their having volunteered for service on the Gold Coast, where malarial fever was known to be a more insidious and more deadly foe than the hordes of barbarian warriors. As one of their number has recorded:

Yet even they were dispirited and disgusted long before blue water was reached. Sent to sea in a ship whose berths were being painted twelve hours before they had to be slept in, through whose cabin floors bilge-water oozed, which was absurdly underhanded for all purposes of attendance, was reeking with foul smells below and flooded above owing to the absence of bulwarks—the passengers in the West African Company's steamship *Ambriz* were as miserable as they could be made. Far from laying in a stock of vigour and energy from the three weeks' voyage, one after another complained that they were being poisoned; and the discomforts suffered in the Bay of Biscay are looked back upon now as exceeding any that the campaign itself induced. (*A Narrative of the Ashanti War*, by Henry Brackenbury.)

All things come to an end, even a long voyage in an unpleasant ship, and on September 27th the *Ambriz* arrived at Sierra Leone, and Wolseley formally took over the command of Her Majesty's forces in the West of Africa settlements. The *Ambriz* then continued the journey, and Cape Coast was reached on October 2nd.

By this time an Ashanti Army of about forty thousand men was encamped within four or five hours' march either of Cape Coast Castle or of the neighbouring settlement of Elmina. No time was to be lost, and two days after his arrival the commander-in-chief held a reception of all the local kings and chiefs, to whom he explained how it was that he had arrived to help them against their common enemy, and how he must depend upon their loyal assistance in punishing the powerful Ashantis.

We are not here concerned with the story of this war except in so far as it is connected with the life-story of our hero. Captain Buller, I have said, was appointed Deputy-Assistant-Quartermaster-General on Colonel Wolseley's Staff, but to him also was entrusted the onerous position of chief of the Intelligence Department.

In this position Captain Buller set to work with characteristic energy and devotion; he had indeed, as no machinery existed for obtaining any information on the spot, to create an Intelligence Department, and at once entered heart and soul into the difficult task. He began by forming a corps of interpreters for service at headquarters, and with the officers who were told off to act as commissioners to the native kings and chiefs—a corps rendered vitally necessary from the fact that the campaign was, if possible, to be fought entirely with native soldiers. Captain Buller left no stone unturned in his efforts to gain trustworthy information from traders or from other people who knew anything of the interior:

> By bribes, by promises, and by threats gently administered, he succeeded in learning something from disaffected Elminas. He examined all the Ashanti prisoners previously in captivity or brought in from our outposts; and he set to work to obtain spies from among the Elminas, and from the Assins, the only people capable of speaking Ashanti without betraying themselves as strangers.

By dint of hard work, sparing neither himself nor others in his zealous greed for necessary information, the indefatigable chief of the Intelligence Department was able to make a useful report to the leader of the Expedition very shortly after they had set to work at Cape Coast. In the course of this report he said:—

> Great endeavours have been made to obtain trustworthy spies and scouts. At Elmina, two women and a boy have brought some valuable information, and one bold and apparently trustworthy Assin has been of use in the eastern district. Pressure having been put upon the Fanti chiefs, they have sent out numerous scouts in their own districts, but the information thus obtained is for the most part not to be relied upon.
>
> Many escaped prisoners of the Ashantis have come in, but the information to be obtained from them is most meagre; the constant fear of death under which they have lived seeming to have frightened all memory out of them. No offers, either of

gold to the poor, place to the ambitious, or freedom to the prisoners can induce anyone to approach the Ashanti camp, such a step being regarded as certain death.

This report shows of itself that the chief of the Intelligence Department had by no means a sinecure in his post, but events certainly proved that Captain Buller was the right man for the work. In carrying out the duties of his branch he "exhibited traits of character" to use the words of Mr. (now Sir) Henry M. Stanley:

Which on a more intimate acquaintance with them will prove him not unworthy of filling posts of the most onerous and most responsible nature.

How true a prophet was the celebrated war correspondent has been proved over and over again in the quarter of a century which has elapsed since those words were written, and is now being seen anew in South Africa.

By the way, a rather good story occurs in Sir Henry M. Stanley's history of the Ashanti war, *apropos* of special correspondents. The present commander-in-chief (Field-Marshal Lord Wolseley) has always had the reputation of being somewhat averse to newspaper correspondents, and another officer on his staff seems to have been no less strenuously opposed to them. The blunt outspokenness of his opinions is indeed suggestive that the officer referred to may have been Buller himself.

A gentleman on Sir Garnet Wolseley's staff, during an argument with me relating to this very subject, and who thoroughly shares Sir Garnet's hatred for newspaper men, when it was suggested to him by me that if Sir Garnet in a European war merely trusted in a correspondent's honour not to mention anything that would furnish information to the enemy, no *gentleman* of the press would disappoint him, blurted out, 'Trust in his honour! By heaven! I would trust to nothing less than his back. On the first publication of anything that I thought not proper, I would tie him to the triangle and trust to fifty lashes well laid on his bare back not to do the like again.' (H. M. Stanley's *Coomassie*.)

Shortly after the arrival at Cape Coast Castle it became necessary to destroy one or two villages near Elmina, both to cut off supplies for the enemy's great camp, and to encourage the Fantis (our native allies). A small body of Houssas and soldiers of the West Indian Regi-

A British Infantryman

ment, a few bluejackets, and some marines, were landed secretly at Elmina on October 14th, and moved towards the village of Essaman. At the moment of landing our hero had a narrow escape from drowning, the boat in which he was carried taking close upon two hours in getting from the ship to the shore, and being very nearly swamped on the way. Captain Buller, who had under his immediate command thirty native labourers armed with axes to help clear the narrow path through the bush, was the first to penetrate through and get a glimpse of the village.

The native troops began by firing wildly, and indicated something of the difficulty, if not the impossibility of keeping to the British Government's instructions of carrying the war through without any large force of white troops. The enemy opened a heavy fire, but despite this General Wolseley's object was at length gained and Essaman destroyed, though not without several casualties. The colonel on the Staff was badly wounded, and Captain Buller took his place, while Buller himself had a narrow escape, a slug penetrating the leather case in which he carried his compass and damaging the instrument. Besides Essaman two other villages were destroyed, and the commander of the Expedition became convinced of the necessity of employing white troops, and also learned something of the power of endurance which such troops possessed in this supposed deadly land. His men had had to march twenty-one miles through a very densely grown country, under a burning sun, and after having been up all night—yet there were but two cases of sunstroke.

Shortly after this brief tentative expedition to Essaman Captain Buller fell a victim to the scourge of the West African climate, and suffering from a sharp attack of malarial fever had to be removed to H.M.S. *Simoon*, which was stationed off the coast as a hospital ship. More fortunate than some others, Captain Buller pulled through the sickness in a short time, and was soon back at his post, the duties of which, during his period of enforced absence, had been performed by Captain (now General Sir) William F. Butler, who had just arrived from home as a special service officer at the time that Buller was stricken down. Captain Butler, it may be added, had performed distinguished service in the Far West, supplementary to that of the Red River Expedition.

Captain Buller was one of the first of the officers to penetrate to the River Prah—the Rubicon between Cape Coast and Coomassie, and a ghastly sight it was which met his eyes along the "road." The original pathway, for it was nothing more, had been widened by the passage of the Ashanti hosts which retired on their own country as the British Expedition advanced; dead bodies lay on the wayside and sometimes in the middle of the path—bodies often of slaves sacrificed to the local fetish that it might keep back the English force; at every mile or so, too, there were clusters of foul-smelling huts.

Like some monster of fable, the Ashanti Army dragged itself homeward to its lair, wounded and weary, leaving behind it a loathsome trail of filth and blood.

This gruesome path had to be widened, and in marshy places to be levelled up and streams to be bridged before an attack could be contemplated upon King Coffee's stronghold. By the end of December, 1873, it could be announced that the main route to the Prah River was reopened; that it was once again the "Queen's highway," no longer a mere bush track, but a broad and spacious road with firm tracks across the marshes and bridges across the rivers.

The campaign was indeed one beset with many difficulties, the most serious being those encountered by the Intelligence and Transport Departments. Roads had to be made, carriers had to be employed by many hundreds over and over again, and from distant districts, and even then, they disappeared as rapidly by desertions as they were secured. Bit by bit, however, the requisite information was acquired, and then as reinforcements arrived from England a move forward could be made. The Headquarters Staff dined together for the last time at Cape Coast Castle on Christmas Day, most of them starting on the road to Coomassie on the following day and the rest of them with General Wolseley on December 27th. The march lay through a country covered with the densest forest and undergrowth which, beautiful as it was when first seen, became, as one who attended the Expedition has recorded, horribly depressing in its terrible monotony:

One may travel for hours in the forest without hearing a sound; for days without seeing anything larger than an insect. It is the absence of sunlight and of that vegetation which requires much sunlight nourishment, which causes this dearth of life.

At the end of January came the first pitched fight with the enemy at the Battle of Amoaful when, after a very trying struggle, the British officers had the satisfaction of knowing themselves to be victorious. General Wolseley had planned carefully, and his Staff worked with un-

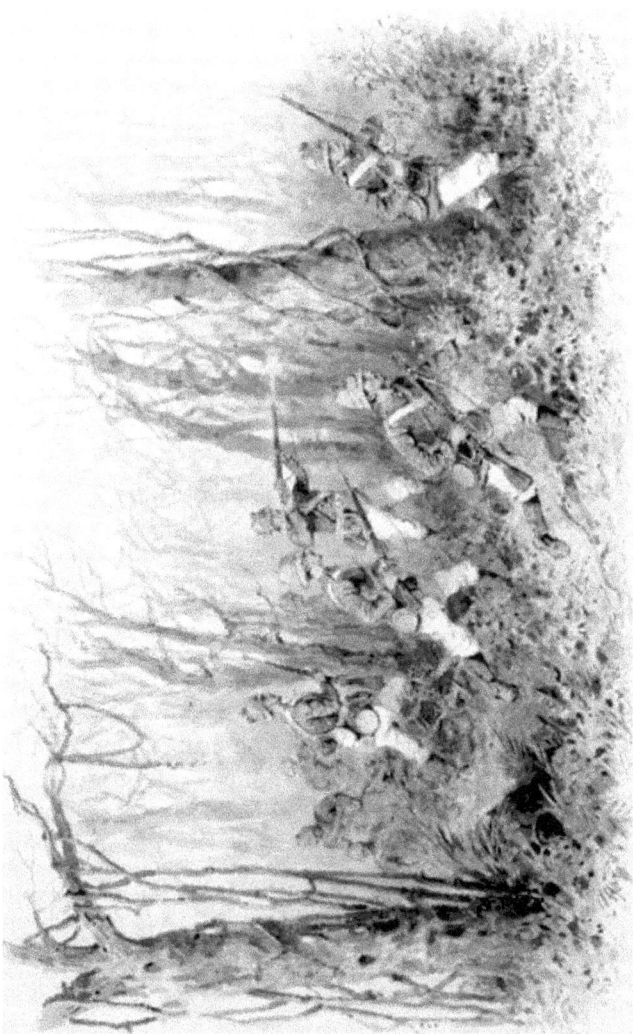

Skirmishing in the Third Anglo–Ashanti War

tiring courage and zeal; Captain Buller, says one describer of the battle, being kept trotting backwards and forwards with orders and reports until it was feared that he would over-exert himself in the strenuous work. At length, however, courage and zeal had its reward, and the day was won.

In making his report to the War Office, it is interesting here to note that the commander named Captain Buller as being one of those officers from whom he had received the most valuable assistance.

After the first day's serious fighting at Amoaful—the first of the five days which led up to the capture of Coomassie—the white troops and native irregulars were led forward to Jarbinbah, where but slight resistance was offered, the advanced guard succeeding in dislodging the enemy. Captain Buller accompanied the advanced guard, which left Amoaful at daybreak on February 2nd, and briefly reported to his chief from Jarbinbah as follows, at half-past eight the same morning:

> Adwabin next. The guide is so positive that Ashantis would be gathered at Adwabin, at the meeting of the Becqua Road, that I go on to tell M'Leod. At present rate of advance we shall be at Adwabin by noon. The brigadier (Sir Archibald Alison) has authorised Colonel M'Leod to put the Rifle Brigade in front, as latter complained of excessive waste of ammunition by Russell's Regiment (composed of natives). Colonel M'Leod estimates the force driven hence at 1,000—they fled west

The estimate proved to be incorrect, for it was after noon when the advanced guard arrived at the village of Agemmamu, little more than half-way to Adwabin. From that place Captain Buller returned to report to General Wolseley, and was sent still further back to Amoaful to bring up the convoy. The energetic head of the Intelligence Department was thus kept busily at it—covering the road to Coomassie twice over in effect. At the next brush with the enemy, at Ordahai, Captain Buller had the misfortune to be wounded—although but slightly, for he was able to take part in the final march on and capture of Coomassie, and in the release of a large number of King Coffee's intended victims, and was well enough to sit up all through the night performing the somewhat exacting duties of a prize agent—taking note of the valuable "loot" which fell into the hands of the Expedition.

But a brief stay was made in the "capital" of Ashanti, and then began the return to the coast. The purpose for which the Expedition set out had been accomplished. King Coffee had signed a treaty of peace, and it behoved those responsible for the British members of the force to get them away from the fatal climate of the West Coast of Africa with as little delay as possible.

On the close of the campaign the commander of the Expedition sent a full report to the Secretary of State for War, in which he warmly eulogised his deputy-assistant-quartermaster-general in the following words:—

> The duties of the Intelligence Department were most efficiently performed by Captain Buller, D.A.Q. M.G. He is an excellent Staff officer. I am much indebted to him for the information of the enemy's doings that he supplied me with throughout the war. The extensive knowledge he acquired of the native tribes both in Ashanti and the territories allied to us, was invaluable to me in my dealings with the kings and chiefs.

When Cape Coast Castle was reached, on February 19th, and before the officers and men began to sail for home, the "loot" from Coomassie was displayed in the local Transport Office previous to being sold—the proceeds being divided up as prize-money. Captain Buller was one of the three prize agents, as I have said, and he and his colleagues having arranged their stores with considerable taste, these were left "on view" for a day and then the sale began. The natives were the chief bidders for the stuffs and beads, but when the gold objects and curios were sold Captain Buller, who was perched on a table as auctioneer, found his fellow-officers keenly competing for their possession. The loot sale realised between three and four thousand pounds.

Buller returned to England with Wolseley and his Staff in the steamship *Manitoban*, which arrived at Spithead on March 20, 1874. An enthusiastic reception awaited all who had taken part in the war, and who, despite all croaking prognostications, had brought it to a successful termination, with a list of casualties which was, all the circumstances considered, not a heavy one. On the last day of March all the officers and troops were inspected by Her Majesty the Queen at Windsor, and Major Redvers Buller—for he was now promoted—received the decoration of a Companion of the Bath. On the evening of the same day the officers of the Expedition were all entertained at a great civic banquet by the Lord Mayor of London.

On April 8th the good people of Crediton gave a, cordial welcome home to Major Buller, when he was presented with a congratulatory address upon his achievements and upon his safe return. In reply the soldier made a brief speech, in which he thanked the inhabitants of Crediton very much for the kind welcome which they had given him. Such an address as they had been pleased to present him with would be valuable to him coming as it did from friends and neighbours, men of the parish in which he was born. Travelling, as he had been, in almost every part of the world, he had never seen men that hung together so well as the men of Devonshire. He remembered that it had been said that

> *When good Queen Bess*
> *Got in a mess,*
> *She sent for a Devonshire man.*

Sir Garnet Wolseley was allowed to select his own Staff, and three out of the four officers he took were Devonshire men, two of whom, he was happy to say, had lived to return. It had been stated in some of the papers that the war was a very iniquitous one, and ought never to have been entered into. All he could say was that he was perfectly shocked with the sight that met his eyes on entering Coomassie. Headless men were strewed in the roadway to impede the progress of the troops. It chanced to be his luck to release the prisoners whom he found, about fifty in number, tied to trees in a place about twenty feet square, perfectly naked, half starved, and waiting every minute to be beheaded. They released them not without some difficulty, because the poor fellows hung around their necks in order to express their gratitude for their timely deliverance. If nothing else had been done, he thought this was a sufficient compensation for the trouble that had been taken and the expense that had been incurred.

CHAPTER 2

Buller's Light Horse

On October 13, 1874, Major Buller, on the death of his eldest
brother, who had never married, inherited the family estates of
Downes, near Crediton, and Cowick and Hayes Barton, near Exeter,
of both of which places he became lord of the manor. Thenceforward,
during such intervals as he has been allowed, he has spent as much
time as possible on his estates, where, it may surprise some people to
learn, he has an enthusiasm for farming, counting among his "hob-
bies" agriculture and stock-raising. He is said to indulge in these hob-
bies with characteristic thoroughness, and to have a sound judgment
on crops, horses, and cattle. He is said too—and this also is eminently
characteristic of the man—always to maintain that the products of his
land are unrivalled, and that he has some grounds for priding himself
on the subject is proved by the frequency with which products of his
estate have figured in the prize lists of agricultural shows.

Our interest, however, centres in him more as a military " man and
leader of men " than as a country gentleman, and we find that he took
a further step up the ladder of promotion in the year after his return
from the West Coast of Africa, when he was chosen for the post of
Deputy-Assistant-Adjutant-General, the first of many responsible War
Office appointments which he was to hold. In the office, as in the
field, he soon got a reputation with those with whom he was brought
into contact, of being a "thorough" man—one who, if he gives an order, expects to see it performed as rapidly and as efficiently as can be.
Many people indeed give him the character of being a severe man—a
disciplinarian of the sternest type, but if he be so he is only severe
where severity is called for, and that is how it is that he has been noted
for the ready and admiring obedience which those under him have
shown. This trait, as we shall see, was especially brought into promi-

nence when he had the difficult task of organising and leading the body of irregular cavalry known as the Frontier Light Horse, which played so brilliant a part in the Kaffir and Zulu Wars.

Early in 1878 the Kaffir rebellion, or the rebellion of the Gaika and Galeka tribes under the old chief Sandilli, assumed such threatening proportions in South Africa, that a number of British troops, as well as Colonial irregulars and levies of friendly natives, were employed in putting it down. Major Buller, whose *fidus achates*, Colonel Evelyn Wood, was engaged in it, volunteered his help, and reached Natal in April, 1878, "on special service." He at once took command of the Frontier Light Horse, a body that had been originally raised by an officer of the 24th Regiment, but which was henceforward, for a couple of years, to be closely identified with the fortunes of Redvers Buller. The corps which had always been a good one, became a remarkably efficient body of men under the inspiriting control of its new leader.

No detail was too small to claim Buller's attention, no work too hard which tended to the improvement of his force, and it has been recorded that he would spend hours in getting saddles that properly fitted the horses so as to prevent any danger of sore backs. To what a pitch of excellence he brought this corps is not only seen in the records of this Kaffir War during the first half of 1878, but also in the more serious Zulu War, which broke out a few months later.

Testimony to the usefulness of the corps and to the prestige which it got under Buller's guidance is found in the fact that when he took it over it numbered but about a couple of hundred men, whereas while under his command he brought the number up to close upon eight hundred. A friendly pen has left an account of the appearance and equipment of the body that came to be known as Buller's Light Horse, and that description is especially interesting at the present time, when similar bodies of Colonial horsemen are actively employed in the war in which Sir Redvers Buller is now engaged over parts of the same country as that in which he distinguished himself twenty years ago.

The first requisite of Buller's Horse was a well-built, sober, and intelligent horseman, who, in addition to being able to shoot with the Martini-Henry, knew also how to groom, saddle, and nurse his steed. This was required to be an animal neither leggy, long-tailed, nor showy, but a clever cobby sort of quadruped, who could climb like a cat, and obey its master like a well-broken spaniel, endued with a sound constitution, stout and wiry, and with a good turn of speed. The saddlery was, as far as possible, of a uniform pattern, and selected with

A KAFFIR CHIEF

considerable judgment and care. The great points were that the tree should be wide enough in the fork not to pinch the shoulders, but yet not so wide as to let the saddle right down on the withers, with the seat long enough to sit in comfortably, and to spread the weight to some extent over the horse's back.

As many of the Cape horses are buck-jumpers, slightly padded flaps were in vogue, although not insisted upon. They are a great protection to the knees in riding through bush. The saddle, of course, was provided with wallets in front, which contained a couple of pairs of socks, one flannel shirt, a toothbrush, towel, and piece of yellow soap. Saddle-bags were worn only when going on distant expeditions, but a tin mug, knife, fork, and spoon, revolver, and flint and steel formed the invariable equipment of these troopers, and with a cloak or blanket *à discrétion* made up the weight carried by the horse. Although the mounted infantry were volunteers drawn from various line regiments, there was sufficient leaven of the cavalry element to insure efficiency in the mounted duties.

When the corps was first raised any kind of dress was worn, but fashion subsequently exerted its sway and a rather picturesque "get up" became almost universally adopted. Broad-leaved felt hats, with coloured *puggarees*, brown cord breeches, "baggy" to the last degree, and so patched with untanned leather that the original material had almost disappeared; a sort of patrol jacket, all over pockets, dyed mimosa colour, and also patched with leather of any colour on the shoulders, and wherever the gun was accustomed to rest, brown laced gaiters coming high up the leg, and even thighs, and a rough coloured flannel shirt, entirely open at the neck: such was the most usual costume. The rifles were of various patterns—long Martinis, Martini-Henry carbines, some of Sharpe's old pattern Sniders and Snider carbines.

Such, so far as words will describe it, was the outward appearance of the Frontier Light Horse as organised by Major Redvers Buller. Not perhaps showy as regards equipment, but eminently serviceable and equal to any amount of unvarying hard work; and for such work it was destined to win a high character. Buller's Light Horse became imbued with something of the endurance and something of the unswerving courage of the officer commanding them.

He was a splendid worker, and never seemed to tire, however great the amount of hard work; and wherever the stiffest place was he was sure to be found. In action, if you could ascertain for certain where most bullets were flying, you would be pretty safe in reckoning that Buller would be in the middle of it.

So, said Mr. F. N. Streatfield, a magistrate on the Kaffrarian border, who commanded a body of Fingoes (*i.e.*, friendly Kaffirs) during the war, and whose story of how he first met Buller is well worth repeating, for it gives some idea of the life then experienced by the leader of the Frontier Light Horse. Streatfield, too, it may be mentioned, was an old Eton boy of Buller's time at school, though they had not known each other then, being in widely separated classes.

When Streatfield had sent a message to Major Buller, he found that his messenger was the only man who knew the way to where the Frontier Light Horse were encamped, and as he and his men had to proceed to join them in the dark, and to travel through a "bush" that might be thick with hidden Kaffirs, he had not an easy task, but he succeeded in accomplishing it. How he did so, and the story of his meeting with his old but hitherto unknown schoolfellow, may best be given in his own words:

We lost the path innumerable times when in the open, and the whole column had to halt while the leading men 'felt' for it. Thus, we got on slowly, slowly, till I was almost beginning to think it was a hopeless case, and that we really should never find Major Buller's camp before daylight came. However, at length, to my inexpressible relief, we saw the reflection of a fire in the distance, and on getting up a bit found it was made by some of the Frontier Light Horse, and that Buller himself was close by. This fire had been made in a hollow, and was totally invisible to anyone down in the forest.

Buller soon heard my voice, and came to meet me. There were men, rolled in their blankets, lying all over the place, and with great difficulty and circumspection I picked my way to him, not, however, without coming a most frightful cropper over one man, whom, I trust, I did not hurt. I was warmly congratulated by Buller on having completed our march successfully, for he knew what sort of a time we must have had. I had told the men to lie down where they were for the few remaining hours, before we moved down to the plateaus, for it was already twelve o'clock.

Buller was sharing a patrol tent with Captain M'Naghten of the Frontier Light Horse, and asked me to crawl in between them, which I was only too glad to do, being miserably cold and wet. I got in quickly, and did not wake M'Naghten. Poor fellow! little did I think as I lay beside him that night that he was having his last sleep in this world! The next night his body was being taken into King William's Town on a bullock waggon with some other men, shot in the attack of the day that was already begun.

The men were situated on a plateau and were about to make a third attack on the Kaffir stronghold of the Perie. Before dawn Major Buller was up and roused his men of the Light Horse, and they and the Fingoes whom Commandant Streatfield had brought with him were soon beginning to move. The attack was a daring one, for it was on a plateau known to be crowded with the enemy, and it was hoped to dislodge them by a rush. The Kaffirs had, however, shifted their ground, and had got among a lot of scattered rocks at the edge of the bush, whence, from places of comparative safety they could shoot the attackers. Captain M'Naghten, mentioned above, was one of the first to fall, shot instantly dead, while another captain of the same corps fell directly afterwards severely wounded.

Buller and a fellow-officer at once headed a few white volunteers and Fingoes, and in the most dashing manner rushed right in among the rocks, and getting under the same cover close to the Kaffirs, shot many of them down and put the rest to flight by sheer daring, for their numbers were vastly inferior to the enemy. Two men were shot during the rush, and Buller himself had a very narrow escape. Thus, the fighting went on for a whole day, and before the next night was more than half through the troops had to be at it again for fear the lurking enemy should still be in the neighbourhood, anywhere in the dense "cover" of the bush. During this day, too, Commandant Streatfield managed to sprain his ankle rather severely, and the accident brought out a fresh trait in the character of the indefatigable leader of the Frontier Light Horse, for to use the words of the officer whom he befriended:

> Buller most kindly rushed about and worked like a brick with my men, making me feel quite jealous of the masterly way in which he came out as a Fingo leader, and showing clearly that his practice with the natives in Ashanti had not been thrown away.

The leader of the Kaffir rebels was, as I have already said, the Gaika chief Sandilli—an old man who, it may be added, had been actively concerned in two earlier rebellions. News reached Buller of the supposed whereabouts of Sandilli, and he at once devised a bold scheme for routing him out of his stronghold in the rocky side of a mountain in the Perie forest. His scheme was neither more nor less than to march during the early night and sleep in the "bush" on the very ground most frequented by the enemy. A bold leader rarely wants for bold followers, and not only the Frontier Light Horse but the native contingent of Fingoes readily followed the hazardous plan. The camping-place reached, parties of Fingoes were sent to discover the "*spoor*" (*i.e.*, footmarks) of the Kaffirs, and these were ultimately found to lead to an absolutely impregnable position, where, entirely hidden from attack, the enemy could shoot every man who approached the entrance to their retreat through the piled-up rocks.

Not to be foiled, and conscious that the capture of Sandilli would mean the collapse of the war, Buller sent for further reinforcements from the neighbouring camp, so that the place might, so far as the nature of the country would permit, be completely surrounded. Buller and one party stayed at the top of the precipitous rock during the following night, at the spot where the traces of the Kaffirs' feet showed that they had descended where a chamois might have hesitated. Lying on a flat rock the officer and his men waited in vain for any sign of the enemy, and in the morning joined the party guarding the foot of the place. Not a sign of the enemy could be seen, and an old prisoner was sent forward as a "feeler."

He was watched anxiously by the English officers and their men for a while, but at length Buller's impatience got the better of his discretion, and he exclaimed—

"Oh, hang it! let's go and take our chance."

Forward he and his companion officers went, followed closely by their men. Scrambling and climbing, now over, now under, the piled-up rocks, "making progress at about a yard a minute" towards the narrow inlet, the foolhardy storming party were somewhat astonished at receiving no volley of shot by way of welcome. The secret was soon out. What had appeared to be the face of the precipice was only the face of a great rock-fall, between which and the cliff itself was a narrow, hidden passage through which the besieged Kaffirs had during the night-time "silently stolen away."

It had been a bold stroke, but an unsuccessful one, and Buller and those under his command had to return to their camp and hope for better luck next time. Several days were spent in "beating" the forest for the enemy who, however, had been effectually dislodged. Two or three days were spent in King William's Town, and then back to camp again, where, however, for some weeks, there was little but routine work to be done, the Kaffirs having totally disappeared from the district. Then news of Sandilli's death was received during the early summer, so that the war was practically over. This being so, in June Major Buller was ordered to proceed north to Natal, leaving the English officers of the native levies to regret the absence of a kindly chief and a cheery friend who, as one of them has recorded, added greatly to the usually scant comfort and happiness of camp life with the Fingoes.

The Kaffir War had been a short one, and Major Buller had only had about three months' work in it when he received these orders to proceed further north, where matters were ripening for the Zulu War. Indeed, a conflict with Cetewayo and his people seemed inevitable, and it was only by the exercise of great tact on the part of Sir Theophilus Shepstone that the peace was kept until the Kaffir rebellion was over. Lord Chelmsford, who had commanded in Kaffraria, was busy in Natal preparing against a possible invasion of the colony by the Zulus, and also preparing, if need should arise, to carry the war into the enemy's country. Major Buller's experience of three months' roughing it after Kaffirs in the bush was to stand him in good stead in the more formidable task on which he was about to enter, while the practice he had had in the organisation and manipulation of the Frontier Light Horse was to make that body an invaluable auxiliary in the approaching conflict.

GENERAL PLAN OF THE OPERATIONS IN ZULULAND, 1879.

Chapter 3

The Zulu War

The Zulu War of 1879 introduces us to a particularly interesting period in Buller's career, for it was in one of the actions of that war that he gave such remarkable evidence of his great personal courage as won for him the coveted honour of the Victoria Cross, and also of his ability as a leader in being able to remove his men with the minimum of loss from a terrible position where the slightest hesitation on his part would have meant the annihilation of his force at the hands of a savage enemy.

During the autumn of 1878, while they were preparing for eventualities, Redvers Buller received further promotion, being gazetted a colonel on November 11th.

When troubles first arose between the British South African Colonies and Zululand during 1878, and Cetewayo—to employ the generally accepted spelling of his name—proved truculent, it finally became necessary for the defence of Natal to adopt an offensive policy and to invade Zululand. In December, the British demands were formulated and the Zulu King was given until the last day of the year to comply with them; a further "ultimatum" was sent in the beginning of January, and no satisfaction being obtainable armed action became inevitable. Lord Chelmsford was in command of the British forces, which he divided into four columns, each of which, while acting independently, was to keep in touch with those nearest to it. The extreme left column was placed under the command of Colonel Evelyn Wood, V.C., and part of his force consisted of the Frontier Light Horse, then about two hundred strong, under Brevet-Lieutenant-Colonel Buller, to give him his official designation at the time.

The headquarters of the left column were at Utrecht, the most southerly town in the Transvaal, and near the point where that country joins both Natal and Zululand. From here the force moved on September 7th with the object of getting sufficiently near to Rorke's Drift to support the next column in the event of an expected Zulu attack. After encamping at Sandspruit, Wood's entire force—all but a small guard left behind—paraded in the lightest possible order early in the afternoon of September 10th, and marched for four hours, when a halt was made until an hour and a half after midnight, "when by the light of a glorious moon the advance was pursued." A short halt was made at three o'clock, when a reconnaissance was ordered in which Buller's Horse took a principal part.

By eight o'clock this advanced body was comfortably encamped within ten miles of Rorke's Drift; they then returned ten miles to the main body and encamped. Within twenty-four hours the men had marched thirty-one miles, but were not long to enjoy the comfort of the camp, for when they were settled for the evening a sudden thunderstorm of terrific force broke over them. Tent-poles snapped and tents collapsed, and in a quarter of an hour the men were up to their ankles in water.

Such unpleasantnesses were, however, the mere incidents of campaigning, and could not be allowed to interfere with any of the serious work in hand, and soon after daybreak next morning (12th) Buller paraded a patrol of his men and took them out, reports having come in from scouts that great numbers of cattle were in the neighbourhood, and the enemy, presumably, not far off. Shortly after they had left the camp they were fired on, but the Zulus did not hold their ground, and the patrol brought in a herd of nearly a thousand head of cattle. Thus, they moved forward with occasional skirmishes for several days, until General Wood was forced to return towards the Umbolosi River by the news which reached him of the terrible disaster which had overtaken the third column at Isandhlwana.

Another column was rendered inactive by being forced to remain in camp at Ekowe, and Wood's was in fact the only available force for some time which could act on the offensive. For several days there was marching and counter-marching without any meeting with the enemy in force. At length, when encamped at a place called Kambula, the commanding officer decided to raid a *kraal* thirty miles away, known as one of the chief rallying-points of the Zulus and as having large quantities of supplies for their army.

The story of this raid admirably illustrates Buller's quiet daring where the opportunity occurs for an adventure of some moment. At four o'clock on the morning of February 1st he selected 106 of the best mounted men from his Frontier Light Horse and thirty-three of the Dutch Contingent under Commandant Piet Uys, and paraded them before the leader of the column. Before starting Buller straightforwardly explained to his troop the details of the feat which they were about to attempt, without in any way seeking to minimise the danger which they would necessarily incur in the performance of an extremely difficult and hazardous duty. The scene is said to have been a most dramatic one, as the camp lanterns lit up the faces of the bronzed and stalwart volunteers who formed the devoted band. The historians of the Zulu campaign say:

> Each man was exceedingly well horsed, and no precaution had been neglected in the careful overhauling of arms, accoutrements, and saddlery. Biscuit and, for those who cared, a little ration of rum were served out, and with a hearty 'God-speed' from their comrades, who half envied their chances of adventure, the little troop of 141 gallant fellows started long before the earliest streak of dawn. The utmost silence was ordered and maintained, while the ground for some miles was so favourable that the horses' hoofs were scarcely heard as they cantered over the light and springy *veldt*.
>
> Distances on horseback are so differently estimated out in South Africa and at home in England, that when the ground is favourable, very long, and to European experience almost impossible, marches are constantly made without distress to horse or rider. In the present instance two short off-saddles only were indulged in; the first not far from the centre of the flat, and the next after the Mangana River had been safely crossed. The country now became more broken and the pace was reduced to a walk, but before the sun was well up the goal was in sight, and the herds of cattle were seen calmly feeding on the slopes. No suspicion would seem to have been excited, and it is more than probable that the very smallness of the attacking force, and its being all composed of the mounted branch, contributed to the success of the affair. The *kraal* was exceedingly well built, and, seen from a distance of 1,200 or 1,000 yards, it was doubtful whether it held a large guard or not. Cautiously, yet swiftly advancing, Colonel Buller felt his way, with a few of his best shots thrown out as vedettes. These men soon encountered

some scattered Zulus, who did not seem at all prepared for any hostile demonstration, but on retiring towards the hills they were reinforced by several other larger bodies, who had evidently been sent out to reconnoitre.

After a few shots had been fired a sudden and simultaneous advance was made on two sides of the *kraal*, and almost without resistance on the part of its defenders the *kraal* was captured. Two hundred and fifty well-built huts were counted by Buller's men, who, losing not a moment, collected no less than four hundred head of cattle, and a large quantity of grain, and then set fire to the magazine. Six Zulus were killed in the capture of the place, and although more than one body of them were seen hovering about in the vicinity, numbering severally 100 to 200 and 300 men, no opposition was offered to the rearguard or patrols." (*The Story of the Zulu Campaign*, by Major Waller Ashe and Captain the Hon. E. V. Wyatt Edgell which has been reprinted by Leonaur in *Anglo-Zulu War of 1879*: Illustrated with maps of the Campaign, and with a *Short Historical Record of the 17th Lancers or Duke of Cambridge's Own During the Zulu War* by J. W. Fortescue.)

The pluck of Buller and his men, aided by the panic which seems to have possessed the defenders of the *kraal*, combined to make the raid remarkably successful. And, indeed, the actual attack was made with a considerably diminished force, because the situation of the kraal, in the centre of a basin surrounded by precipitous hills, rendered it necessary for Buller to leave a material part of his force, thirty men, to guard the pass by which they had come through the hills.

The party returned to their comrades at Kambula without having met with any casualty. At Kambula a strongly entrenched camp was formed, and from it during February and the early part of March several small expeditions were sent out in most of which Buller and his Light Horse played an important part. Although for some time they met with but little opposition from the enemy, they succeeded in capturing large numbers of cattle, and in several of these excursions the leader of the Frontier Light Horse gave fresh evidence of his indomitable endurance, his courage and resourcefulness.

Another particularly noteworthy sortie of a similar character undertaken by Colonel Buller, and carried out with complete success, calls for mention. At ten o'clock at night, on March 14th, a strong detachment of the Frontier Light Horse, along with fifty of the mounted Transvaal Volunteers under Piet Uys, paraded "without lights, bugles, or the slightest sound, and moved off silently into the bush, without even the jingle of a sabre or the clank of a chain," from Colonel Wood's camp at Kambula with the object of destroying the great military *kraal* of Manyanyoba—a *kraal* which the Zulu king, Cetewayo, and his chiefs considered as one of the safest of their strongholds.

Colonel Buller took a gun with him, but before setting out had its wheels carefully swathed in cloth and raw hide to prevent any sound and as a protection against rocky parts of the journey. The gun was got into position and the leader sent his Frontier Light Horse forward on the left with instructions to remain in the bush until they heard the shelling of the *kraal*, when they were to rush out and secure what cattle there might be, driving them round to Piet Uys and his Boers. Just as the sun rose two shells were fired from the gun, and the second burst right in the centre of the *kraal* where the cattle were kept. The frightened Zulus fled, but once on the mountain-side turned and fired at their attackers, though without inflicting any serious damage. The little expedition was entirely successful, and Buller not only destroyed the formidable military centre but took some four hundred head of cattle back to camp, having successfully managed the retreat to headquarters despite the fact that the Zulus were rapidly and numerously reinforced.

At about this time an incident happened at a place some thirty miles from Sir Evelyn Wood's camp, which, although not directly connected with our hero's life-story, is interesting as illustrating his views no less strongly than those of his chief at the time. A convoy of about seventy soldiers with a number of waggons bound for Luneberg had halted for the night at a point about ten miles away, part of the convoy being on either side of the "drift," or fording-place. Suddenly, at four o'clock in the morning, the enemy, four or five thousand strong, fell on the camp and *assegaied* the greater number of the men.

A lieutenant in command, his captain being one of the first to fall, mounted and galloped off to Luneberg for reinforcements, leaving his men to their fate. He was subsequently court-martialled for having gone off on the only horse, leaving his men engaged in a desperate engagement. The court found him "not guilty," but the general commanding, on the proceedings being submitted to him, endorsed them "disapproved and not confirmed," the officer "to be released from arrest, and to return to his duty."

If that were all of the painful incident it would not have called for notice here, but in refusing to confirm the verdict Lord Chelmsford recorded his reasons as follows, and his words were subsequently approved by the commander-in-chief and ordered to be read at the head of every regiment in Her Majesty's service:

Had I released this officer without making any remarks upon the verdict in question it would have been a tacit acknowledgment that I concurred in what appears to me a monstrous theory, *viz.*, that a regimental officer who is the only officer present with a party of soldiers actually and seriously engaged with the enemy can, under any pretext whatever, be justified in deserting them, and by so doing abandoning them to their fate. The more helpless the position in which an officer finds his men, the more it is his bounden duty to stay and share their fortune, whether for good or ill. It is because the British officer has always done so that he occupies the position in which he is held in the estimation of the world, that he possesses the influence he does in the ranks of our army.

The soldier has learnt to feel that, come what may, he can, in the direst moment of danger, look with implicit faith to his officer, knowing that he will never desert him under any possible circumstances. It is to this faith of the British soldier in his officers that we owe most of the gallant deeds recorded in our military annals; and it is because the verdict of this court-martial strikes at the root of this faith that I feel it necessary to mark officially my emphatic dissent from the theory upon which the verdict has been founded.

It is easy to believe that General Buller would cordially endorse every word of that statement made by Lord Chelmsford; indeed, in all too few weeks he was to have a somewhat similar incident immediately under his notice—and an incident which brought from him, as we shall see, much more bluntly emphatic language than that used in Lord Chelmsford's report.

One more of Colonel Buller's important expeditions, from the Kambula camp, somewhat similar to those already mentioned, calls for some description. A brother of Cetewayo's, Oham (or Uhama), had come in and submitted, with three or four hundred of his men, to General Wood, and had begged that his wives and family might be rescued before they could fall into the hands of the king. Twenty of

Oham's men were sent off to collect them, and then, on March 14th, Buller set out once more before daybreak, but with a larger body than usual, consisting of a strong detachment of his own Frontier Horse, a number of the Boer Volunteers under Piet Uys, with a couple of hundred of Oham's men. Sir Evelyn Wood, it may be mentioned, accompanied the party. A member of the Expedition has left us a graphic account of the ride to the caves of Nhlangwine, where the chief's wives and family (and, incidentally, cattle) were collected. These caves were no less than forty-five miles away from the camp, yet Colonel Buller succeeded in his enterprise, and got back to Kambula in safety with close upon a thousand of Oham's people in little more than fifty hours.

They rode along for a considerable time in complete silence, the men being allowed to smoke their pipes, but not to speak above a whisper. At first, they followed the *spoor* of some cattle, which indicated the road by which Oham and, his people had come to the camp, and then, turning more in a northerly direction, followed the course of some small streams which flowed from the hills upon the left. The moon shone brightly, and enabled them to see clearly for some distance before them. Many strange sounds were heard—the growl of some beast of prey, or the scream of the night-birds disturbed by the clank of the horses' hoofs, or the occasional rattle of a chain. The rapidity with which the column cantered over the soft and springy veldt, the dead and ominous silence maintained by all hands, and the steady and business-like mode in which they pursued their course, neither turning to the right nor to the left, gave the journey a singularly weird character.

As soon as the first morning's light began to appear the guides, who rode in front, turned into a ravine covered with dense brushwood and trees, and having ascended this for about three miles, they found it was possible to ride out of it in three different directions, besides the one by which they had entered, and thus a retreat could be effected if any attack were made. Here it was decided to make the first off-saddle and partake of breakfast. At a signal from their leader, and without any word of command, the horsemen dismounted, slackened girths, and took off saddles, while the bits were removed from the horses' mouths and the animals allowed, Cape fashion, to take the customary roll in the grass. This luxury to a Cape horse seems indispensable, and without it he will rarely enjoy his grass or corn. No sooner, however, had the steeds rolled than each was again saddled, and, with the exception of the still slackened girths, was ready to be mounted in half a moment. Rifles and revolvers were carefully examined, to see whether the night-dew had done any mischief, and then, having made a careful sweep round the horizon with his field-glasses, the commander gave the order for the morning meal, which consisted of a little cold tea, some bread, and '*beltong*' (sun-dried game).

After half an hour's rest they again started as before. The day had broken with all the splendour of an African morning. . . . Mounting to the head of the *kloof* the party came to a splendid prospect and panorama stretching out below. . . . Away up a smaller valley on the right lay the path that had to be followed, and, leaving the bright and smiling landscape in front, the column once more plunged into the gloom of the bush. Two more outspans brought them to sunset, and now precautions had to be redoubled, as they were nearing dangerous ground. The chances were more than probable that Cetewayo, on hearing of his brother's defection and flight, had sent a party of his warriors to take possession of his wives and cattle, both vendible commodities in the land. If this were the case, it would inevitably result that a vigilant watch would be kept to prevent their escape to Oham.

Strange to say, these anticipations were only partly verified, for as the troops neared the caves, they could see that they were watched, but only by scattered and weak bodies of Zulus. These fellows had evidently discovered that the white man's intention was hostile, and they probably thought his object was cattle, and not to recover or rescue Oham's wives and children, for they ran rapidly along the heights above, taking no precaution for concealment, and seeming only anxious to drive away their herds. As the horsemen approached the caves at a canter, flankers were extended on either side to prevent surprise. The excitement of Buller's men could hardly be restrained, while the calm and stolid Dutchmen, who glided silently and grimly on, offered a wide contrast to their more hot-blooded comrades.

As they came nearer and nearer the place seemed inhabited, and it was evident that the natives sent on a few days previously had apprised the people of Buller's advent and friendly intentions. Then Oham's people came crowding out of their caves, jostling each other in their anxiety to greet the English soldiers, grasping their *assegais*, and giving vent to a series of guttural clicks, which it would baffle any known, combination of vowels to reproduce. . . . At nine the following morning a compact column was formed, consisting of the rescued allies or prisoners, the few cattle collected in the centre, and the whole party started for the homeward march. It could scarcely have been hoped that the retreat would have been unmolested, yet only at the Mklepgwene, a difficult defile, were they fired upon by a body of Zulus, evidently hastily collected, and numbering some thousand men. The detachment reached the camp with the rescued families at 1 p.m. on the 16th. (*The Story of the Zulu Campaign.*)

This account has seemed worthy of quoting at length as a rare personal record of an expedition which may be taken as typical of the many which Colonel Buller undertook and which won for him not only the devoted admiration of the men whom he led, but also such high commendation from his own commander as to be dubbed his "right hand" during the campaign.

We are now approaching the memorable day when the dashing leader of the Frontier Light Horse was to perform such deeds as were to render his name familiar in our mouths as household words and to win for him the highest honour which can fall to the lot of a soldier—that of the decoration of the Victoria Cross, known by all as the "V.C." After some days of comparative quiet, Colonel Buller was summoned to the tent of his friend and commander, Sir Evelyn Wood, where, with the Boer leader, Piet Uys, a council of war was held to discuss the advisability of attacking a Zulu stronghold on the Inhlobane Mountain. This mountain, an elevated tableland of about three thousand acres, standing 1,200 feet above the surrounding country, formed part of a range of mountains visible from Kambula camp. It was known that the Zulus on the mountain possessed a large number of cattle, and, despite the known difficulties, Buller and Uys were ready and willing for the fresh dangerous undertaking.

At three o'clock the following morning the first portion of the chosen detachment, consisting altogether of four hundred horsemen and three hundred natives, started, Colonel Buller and Piet Uys leading. This party was bound for the north-eastern path up the mountain.

Colonel Buller at Inhlobane

Colonel Russell followed with a second detachment to mount by the nearer western path, and Sir Evelyn Wood and his Staff started shortly after. Absolutely precipitous on its northern and southern sides, the summit was only to be attained by paths from its north-eastern and its western extremities. By the evening the different detachments had all reached the top, which, it must be noted, is about three miles long, and then one of the native allies learned that seven large regiments had left Ulundi, the Zulu capital, three days earlier bound for that district. He told Colonel Wood, and begged that their small force might at once return to Kambula; but this could not be done without exposing Colonel Buller and those who were in front to be cut off and surrounded, so that it was decided that at all risks a junction must be made with them.

At half-past three in the morning Sir Evelyn Wood ordered the word to be quietly passed round, for the men to stand to their horses and prepare to march. The moon now and again broke through the clouds, and so helped them in following the faint traces of the leading party. Distant and desultory firing was heard towards the north-eastern side; then, as the sun rose, they met such signs of the fighting as a broken *assegai*, a damaged shield, then some dead Zulus and the body of a horse. All these signs showed that Buller and his men had passed and had met with some resistance, and hoping that they had already made good their retreat by the other end of the tableland, Sir Evelyn Wood was finally compelled to return with his small party the way they had gone.

Buller had indeed lost a couple of officers and one of his men in attaining the top in the early hours of the morning, and met with some opposition on the plateau, but soon dispersed the enemy and found some two thousand head of cattle which the Zulus had driven up there for safety. He then surveyed the possible descents from the mountain, and decided to use that at the north-western extremity for the retreat of a portion of his force. Returning to the eastern end, Colonel Buller told off his second in command, Captain Barton, with a party of thirty men, to bury the bodies of those killed in the ascent, to find Colonel Weatherley with his small detachment, and return to camp with him by the southern route by which they had come.

Shortly before nine o'clock in the morning and just after Barton's departure, Buller caught sight of the Zulu Army—of which news had reached Colonel Wood—estimated at twenty thousand men, approaching the mountain from the south-east, and then about six miles away. Buller calculated that his force would have an hour's start of the enemy, but realising that the retreat of Barton would be seriously threatened by the Zulu advance, sent a couple of troopers after the captain, telling him that his campward route was to be by the north side of the mountain. The captured cattle had by this time been collected near the western extremity, and to this point Buller at once moved his force. He considered that a descent by the rugged north-western path— that nearest to Kambula, too—would allow the scattered troops on the summit to be united and withdrawn in comparative safety, while they would further gain the support of Colonel Russell's force, which had been directed to approach the plateau from the west.

At ten o'clock Colonel Wood and his staff, returning along the southern base of the mountain to visit Colonel Russell's encampment, became aware of the rapid approach of the Zulu Army, and the commander at once sent a communication to Russell to meet him at a certain point. At the same time Colonel Russell, with his force on a lower plateau of the mountain than Buller, also saw the enemy, and, abandoning the cattle which they had secured, retreated to the foot of the mountain to take up a position on some rising ground to cover Buller's retreat. The English officers, however, had not been the only ones to notice the great army approaching. The numerous Zulus hidden in caves and other cover on the mountain had also seen it, and in ever-increasing numbers harassed the movement of Buller's force towards the western extremity of the plateau.

When the top of the path leading down the cliff was reached the very serious difficulties of the descent became apparent. There was, however, now no alternative, and the dangerous retreat to the lower plateau had to be undertaken. This brought out the leader's masterly qualities. He worked with a marvellous coolness and with almost unexampled bravery in his efforts to get his force away to safety with the least loss. The descent had to be made by a path which has been described as consisting of a series of ledges from eight to twelve feet wide, on which an insecure foothold could be obtained, the drop from one ledge to the next being about three or four feet.

Colonel Buller first sent down the native portion of his force, covering their retreat with the mounted men. These then began to descend, the Frontier Light Horse forming the rearguard, and for a while successfully checking the enemy. The descent was necessarily very slow, and the Zulus succeeded in getting positions above and below the path, whence, sheltered by rocks, they could keep up an

BATTLE OF INHLOBANE

incessant fire on the plucky horsemen. Buller himself was the very last man to descend, and it was in the course of this memorable retreat that he performed those amazing deeds of daring which won for him the Victoria Cross. Those deeds have been often described, but never more clearly than by his commanding officer at the time. Sir Evelyn Wood, in contributing an article on "the Mount of Valour" to *Pearsons Magazine* three years ago, wrote of his friend as follows:—

When the last of the troops had left the plateau, Buller was heard to say to Commandant Piet Uys, who was in command of thirty Dutchmen, 'You go down, Piet; I'll stop up here! And when you get to the bottom halt some men to cover us as we come down.' Turning then to Lieutenant Everitt of the Frontier Light Horse, he ordered him to halt ten men, who, as a covering party, were to descend last of all. Mr. Everitt could only collect seven men, but these kept the Zulus back for some time, descending later with the enemy close upon them; four of the little party were almost immediately killed, and Lieutenant Everitt's horse was *assegaied*.

Buller, a tall and powerful man, now seizing Mr. Everitt, who was exhausted, by the collar of the coat, pulled him out of the way of the pursuing Zulus, who were themselves greatly impeded by the rugged nature of the cliffs, and, standing over his breathless lieutenant, received from him a carbine and ammunition, saying, 'Get on down as quick as you can!' and with the three men remaining alive out of the reaguard of seven, Buller covered the retreat of the last of those descending the cliff....

Buller's command was now demoralised; and one very brave officer of an irregular corps, who had often shown great personal courage, burst into tears when his men refused to obey his order to form up to cover the retreat of the Frontier Light Horsemen, who were still descending the mountain. He himself remained, and assisted Colonel Buller in rallying the men, and had not this been effected, none of the wounded nor those who had lost their horses could have escaped.

Buller himself was ubiquitous, and to my knowledge rescued four men that day, three of whom lived for years afterwards; the fourth man, whom he pulled out of the middle of a struggling crowd of Zulus and carried, holding on to his stirrup, down the hill, was eventually wounded much lower down, and lost his life.

Trooper Randal, Frontier Light Horse, told me five days later that in the retreat his horse was completely exhausted, when he was overtaken by Colonel Buller, who was falling back with the rearmost men, and that the colonel put him up on his own horse and carried him for some distance; then, dropping him, returned again to the fight, this time picking up Captain C. D'Arcy, also of the Frontier Light Horse. This officer had lost both his horses, and when panting along on foot with the Zulus less than a hundred yards behind him was rescued by Colonel Buller, who took him up on his horse.

The first man to ascend the eastern end of the mountain in the grey dawn, Buller acted throughout the retreat as the rearmost man of the rearguard, although he knew from experience that any man who was wounded was sure to be ripped up by the ruthless enemy. . . .

That evening we were sitting in our sodden tents, for the rain was falling heavily. We had seen the Zulu Army bivouacking seven miles off our camp, and while we did not feel doubtful of the result of any open attack, yet our native allies had disappeared, and the 1,800 British soldiers had a stern task awaiting them on the morrow.

Buller and his men had been almost continuously in the saddle for one hundred consecutive hours, during which time they had skirmished once, fought twice, and marched over 170 miles. Nevertheless when, at nine o'clock, a solitary fugitive from a detachment, of which some few men had escaped over the eastern end of the Mhlobane, crawling into camp, reported that half a dozen more stragglers were trying to reach Kambula, the indomitable Buller had no difficulty in immediately mounting a dozen volunteers, whom he led forth on their jaded horses into the pitchy darkness of the night, returning later with the last survivors of the bloody fight of the 28th of March.

The official account of this fine deed, which Buller's fellow-officer so well describes, was given as follows in the *Gazette*, which announced that Colonel Redvers Buller had been awarded the Victoria Cross:—

For his gallant conduct at the retreat at Mhlobane, on March 28, 1879, in having assisted, while hotly pursued by Zulus, in rescuing Captain C. D'Arcy of the Frontier Light Horse, who was retiring on foot, Colonel Buller carrying him on his horse until he overtook the rearguard; also for having on the same day, and in the same circumstances, conveyed to a place of safety Lieutenant C. Everitt of the Frontier Light Horse, whose horse had been killed under him. Later on, Colonel Buller, in the same manner, saved a trooper of the Frontier Light Horse, whose horse was completely exhausted, and who otherwise would have been killed by the Zulus, who were within eighty yards of him.

RESCUING A WOUNDED SOLDIER

CHAPTER 4

The Final Battle

Buller's work in Zululand was not only brilliant in itself, but it forms a highly important phase in his development as a leader, and it is fortunate that we have fuller records of his doings during this South African campaign than of any other of his military services. Many men who were engaged in the Kaffir and Zulu Wars have left striking records of those struggles—records which are fortunately full of personal touches with regard to the soldierly commander of the Frontier Light Horse. His splendid performances on the Mount of Valour mark an epoch in the life of the great General, but his later achievements during the Zulu War are also worthy of full consideration, winning as they did for him the strongest commendation of his superiors in command.

The last chapter closed with the "official" record, the very baldest account of the deed which, however simply described, compels the reader's enthusiastic admiration for the sterling qualities of the courageous soldier. The present chapter opens on the very day after the masterly retreat from the Inhlobane Mountain, and opens on one of the severest battles of the whole campaign. The great Zulu Army of twenty thousand men which had been perceived the day before had made a rapid march from the king's *kraal* with the object of dislodging General Wood's camp of Kambula.

Very few hours' rest sufficed for the brave warriors, and at noon on the following day (March 28th) the Kambula camp was severely attacked by the Zulus, and a very serious battle ensued for some hours, the masses of the enemy being finally beaten and pursued with very heavy losses, Buller and his Frontier Light Horse playing an important part in the fortunes of the day and in the final rout of the Zulus. So thorough was the defeat on this occasion, that there followed a period of comparative quiet in the western parts of Zululand, and Colonel

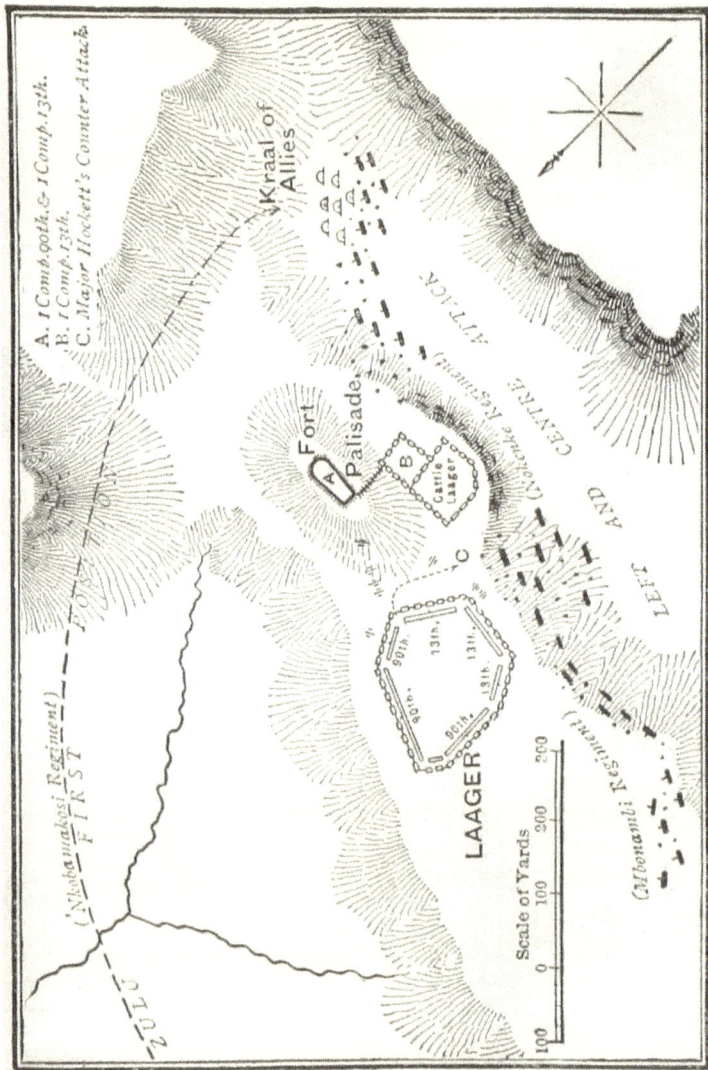

PLAN OF THE BATTLE OF KAMBULA.

A. *1 Comp. 90th. & 1 Comp. 13th.*
B. *1 Comp. 13th.*
C. *Major Hackett's Counter Attack*

Kraal of Allies

CENTRE ATTACK

LEFT AND

(*Nokenke Regiment*)

(*Nodwengu Regiment*)

Fort

Palisade

A

B

Cattle
Laager

C

90th

13th

90th   13th

90th   13th

LAAGER

(*Mbonambi Regiment*)

FIRST

(*Ndabawakosi Regiment*)

ZULU

Scale of Yards

100   0   100   200   300   400

Wood's column had comparatively little to do until the time came for the concerted march on Cetewayo's capital, Ulundi.

A glimpse of our hero as he appeared at Kambula to a newspaper correspondent may fittingly be quoted here before we follow his fortunes on to the fall of the Zulu capital. Mr. Archibald Forbes has written in one of his many volumes of reminiscences:

> When I first visited Wood's camp in Zululand, I found Buller there in command of some 800 volunteer irregular horsemen—or perhaps rather mounted infantry; a strange, wild, heterogeneous band, whom Buller held in sternest discipline, and made do wonders in fighting and marching, by sheer force of character. A stern-tempered, ruthless, saturnine man, with the gift of grim silence not less than a gift of curt, forcible expression on occasion, Buller ruled those desperadoes with a rod of iron. Yet, while they feared him, they had a sort of dog-like love for him.

The same observant correspondent described the men of Buller's force as consisting of men of all—and no—characters, and of all nationalities, and indicates the secret of the officer's unquestioned power over them by describing him as "a silent, saturnine, bloodthirsty man, as resolute a fighter as ever drew breath—a born leader of men." It was just after the fight at Kambula camp, when Sir Evelyn Wood had given such a check to the Zulu power in defeating their army of twenty thousand, that Mr. Forbes visited it, and his descriptions of Buller are interesting as showing us the general of today in process of gaining that knowledge and mastery of men which it may be hoped will now stand him in good stead when he is once more engaged in warfare in South Africa; a stern-tempered, ruthless man, with a gift of grim silence no less than a gift of curt, forcible expression on necessary occasion—such is the impression which the colonel made on the newly arrived war correspondent, and such is, in effect, the description given by most men who have only seen the officer in the field.

The Kambula fight had created the necessary "diversion" to allow of Lord Chelmsford making a strong attempt to break up Cetewayo's power with a final blow, and at length arrangements were made for a general advance. At the beginning of May Lord Chelmsford, with several of his Staff officers and Prince Louis Napoleon (the Prince Imperial), arrived at Kambula, and immediately afterwards a reconnaissance was made and a new camping ground discovered; and then the camp was broken up and the force moved off to a new ground some miles away and close to the boundary between the Transvaal and Zululand. For several months General Wood and Colonel Buller with their men had occupied Kambula, and the place had become to them one of many and honourable memories. Buller's Horse, under their able leader, had by this had a goodly share of varied experience, and were now thoroughly seasoned and fit for any calls that might be made upon them.

Their numbers, too, had grown by reinforcement of several similar troops to as many as a thousand. Before actually beginning the general advance, it was decided that previous to any formidable cavalry patrol being undertaken in force, a series of short reconnaissances should be carried out by the indefatigable Buller and his ubiquitous horsemen. One of these reconnaissances calls for particular mention, if only for the very graphic description which has been left of it by an eye-witness. It started on the night of the 9th of May with General Wood himself in command, the force consisting of but about one hundred and fifty horsemen.

They had gone some miles and it was broad daylight, when a couple of shots in front told them that the enemy were about. Then came a tremendous shout from the rear, and it was found that, true to their usual tactics, the Zulus had let the force go by that they might attack them, unprepared, from behind. General Wood at once ordered a halt, and gave the word for twenty men to wheel about and charge back in full force upon the unsuspecting foe.

> With a hearty English shout these fellows, led by Buller, went straight at the enemy, and bursting over rough ground and through the high and tall grass drove the flying Zulus in panic before them. Buller's appearance at this moment combined an element of the heroic and the terrible, with a strong infusion of the ludicrous and burlesque. Leading his men on at a swinging canter, with his reins in his teeth, a revolver in one hand and a *knobkerrie* he had snatched from a Zulu in the other, his hat blown off in the *mêlée*, and a large streak of blood across his face, caused by a splinter of rock from above, this gallant horseman seemed a demon incarnate to the flying savages, who slunk out of his path as if he had been—as indeed they believed him—an evil spirit, whose very look was death.

The tables were now completely turned; the whole of the column is safely through the *poort*; one or two Zulus are seen limping away, assisted into the bush by their comrades, while the rest stand not upon the order of their going, but rush pell-mell to gain the shelter of the neighbouring caves. One large Zulu is seen to be badly hit, yet he manages to crawl away out of sight, and doubtless is assisted to escape by his fellows.

The fun is becoming fast and furious, Buller's men are in their glory. They have dashed into the *kloof*, and are driving the Zulus out of it in parties of six or eight at a time. Everybody, who an hour ago was as silent and sombre as the grave, thinks it now necessary to yell with excitement. . . . But the chase begins to slacken; the pace is too good to last, the recall sounds, and the firing dies away to a few desultory shots, while the troopers canter back dishevelled and puffing like schoolboys after a hard-won goal at football.

The small party spent a couple of days skirmishing and reconnoitring in the enemy's country, and then returned with useful data to General Wood's camp. After a single day's rest another reconnaissance was decided upon, and again Colonel Buller set out, this time with a couple of hundred picked horsemen, "well-mounted, well-armed, and well-trained," and had with him besides as "guests," the Prince Imperial and several officers from headquarters. With three days' rations the party set out to reconnoitre in another direction, and again they fell in with scattered forces of Zulus, and had some slight skirmishes, but succeeded in getting useful information about the country before returning to the camp on May 16th. On this reconnaissance the young French prince distinguished himself by brave disregard of danger.

At length, at the end of May, matters were nearly ripe for a general advance, and the camp at Wolf's Kraal had to be given up, and Wood's Flying Column of about two thousand men began its forward movement. The Flying Column was attached to General Newdigate's (or the Second) Column, to which it acted as an advanced force, keeping about five miles ahead. In the Flying Column of course "the Rupert of South Africa," as Redvers Buller was called, had a prominent part with his fine body of horsemen ready to follow him anywhere and die for him to a man after his splendid devotion on the Inhlobane Mountain and elsewhere.

On Sunday, June 1st, occurred one of the tragedies of the campaign, when the Prince Imperial, who was attached to the headquarters Staff as a "guest," went out with a small patrolling party and was killed. With the details of this tragic occurrence we are not here concerned, nor are we concerned to discuss the relative share of blame to be attached to the officer who galloped away from the unfortunate prince and to the staff officer who permitted the guest to penetrate into the enemy's country with an insufficient force. The day was a beautiful one, and General Wood had ridden out with an escort, when some fugitive horsemen were seen in the distance. They had not very long to wait for a solution of the mystery, and, riding on, they were met by Colonel Buller and a dozen of his men, no less anxious to discover who the flying horsemen might be.

> They all rode on together, and rounding the base of the cliff came up with Lieutenant Carey and four troopers of Bettington's Horse. In a few seconds more the terrible secret was revealed, and Lieutenant Carey, whose horse was almost dead-beat and covered with foam, was rapidly relating to General Wood the details. 'Where is the prince?' exclaimed Wood, as he breasted his horse at some fallen trees which intervened, and dashed forward to meet the fugitives. 'Speak, sir; what has happened?'—'The prince, I fear, is killed, sir,' said one of the men, Carey being at first unable to speak. 'Is that the case? Tell me instantly, sir,' answered the general. 'I fear 'tis so, general,' was the answer; upon which our chief, 'And what are you, sir, doing here?'

There are several versions of this meeting, several of which strongly illustrate at once Buller's blunt outspokenness and his innate detestation of an act unworthy of a soldier. The following is the story as told by Sir George Pomeroy Colley, the officer who, a couple of years later, was in command at the disastrous reverse on Amajuba Hill. Colley, who had been appointed Chief of the Staff to Lord 'Wolseley (then Sir Garnet Wolseley) when that officer took over the command in Zululand, wrote as follows to his wife:—

> I am afraid the more one hears of the circumstances of the Prince Imperial's death, the more sad and discreditable to our name it appears.
> I had a graphic account of the meeting between an officer who was with him and Buller (from a man who was present. Evelyn Wood ('Sir Evelyn' he is now, I see, and right well he has earned it) and Buller were riding ahead of the column as usual to look

out for good camping ground, when suddenly they saw an officer riding furiously towards them—so furiously that Buller observed, 'Why, the man rides as if he thought the Kaffirs were after him.' As he came nearer, he gesticulated wildly and beckoned to them to go back, but they rode on till they met him. 'Whatever is the matter with you?' said Buller. 'The Prince—the Prince Imperial is killed,' was all the man could gasp out, breathless and wild. 'Where?—where is his body?' asked Buller sharply. The man could only gasp and point to a hill about three miles off, from which they could now see some twenty Kaffirs going away in the opposite direction with three led horses. 'Where are your men, sir? How many did you lose?' said Buller sharply and sternly, now thoroughly roused. 'They are behind me—I don't know,' stammered the unfortunate man. Then said Buller, turning on him savagely, 'You deserve to be shot, and I hope will be. I could shoot you myself,' and turned his back on him.

Had it been either Wood or Buller, they would have turned had it been a thousand Kaffirs, and probably would have brought him away; but this wretched officer seems to have raced with his men who should get away first, and was actually leading his men in their flight, and still galloping wildly, though three miles away from the scene of action.

June was well forward when everything was ready to push on with the advance on the Zulu capital. Buller, as usual, was well to the front; in fact, he and a body of his well-tried horsemen were generally some miles ahead of Wood's Flying Column, which in turn kept about five miles in front of the main body. Buller, indeed, was indefatigable and ubiquitous—to the front, and on either flank, he had patrolled for many miles, dislodging such few Zulus as were found, and gaining simply invaluable data as to the country to be traversed before reaching Cetewayo's *kraal*.

On June 25th Buller and his party, patrolling nine miles ahead, pounced upon some seventy or eighty of the enemy busily engaged in burning the grass, to bother the English advance by destroying food for their horses and oxen. The dashing "Rupert" and his men made short work of the Zulus, and soon put an end to their destructive action, and returned with information respecting five *kraals*, which had been observed guarded by about a thousand Zulus. The next day

133

a small force was sent out to destroy these, and again Buller did yeoman's service. At length, on the 30th of June, the whole column were within a few miles of Ulundi, and an ultimatum was sent to Cetewayo, naming the conditions on which peace negotiations would be entertained, and giving the Zulu king three days in which to decide.

During these days of grace Buller was far from idle, scouring the country in front and on either flank with his men, with the double object of making observations and preventing a surprise on the part of a treacherous enemy. No reply came to Lord Chelmsford's ultimatum, but instead scattered bodies of the enemy kept up an intermittent fire on the English. Colonel Buller therefore asked and obtained permission to make a raid into the enemy's country, which he did on the afternoon of July 3rd, having with him Lord William Beresford and a number of picked horsemen.

They crossed the River Umbolosi, protected by gunfire, and at once dashed after the Zulus on the other side, and soon put them to flight, Buller dividing his men that they might raid different points. With a hundred of his best men he contemplated a rush on Ulundi and a firing of the royal *kraal*, but this "somewhat hare-brained exploit" was prevented by the sudden discovery of numerous Zulus in a hollow just ahead.

Here the Zulu general, whoever he was, had admirably disposed his reserves, and here, but for the steady conduct of all hands, Buller might have met his fate. As suddenly as the mountain warriors of Roderick appeared above the heather to James Fitz-James did the tall Zulu warriors put in an appearance, and from front and flank a very well-sustained fire was poured in upon the daring Buller and his men. But Buller, with all the dash of a Rupert or a Murat, had much of the prescience of a veteran. . . . He had, previously to his daring advance in the enemy's country, ordered Commandant Raaf to halt near Nondwengo with his horsemen as reserves and supports.

At the imminent moment, therefore, when the Zulus appeared in the hollows, these gallant fellows came up and saved the day, and it is more than probable many valuable lives. As Buller and his splendid marksmen retired by alternate ranks, and as each man fired, dropping his man, Raaf and his well-trained fellows covered the slow retreat.

Buller, as before, behaved splendidly in the way in which, placing himself wherever hard knocks were to be obtained, he kept between his men and the oncoming enemy.

One result of this magnificently courageous reconnaissance was to make Lord Chelmsford decide to advance at once upon Ulundi, and to give the enemy every temptation to attack his force between the river and the *kraal*, upon a plain which Buller had marked out during one of his patrols as an ideal battle-ground. Early on the 4th the troops were moved on to this plain and formed ready in square, while Buller with his advanced body of horsemen galloped ahead, firing the *kraals* and tempting the enemy to the attack.

It was known that there was a great force, probably twenty thousand Zulus, in the neighbourhood, and Buller made a strong attack on the left of their main advancing column, adopting tactics similar to those which he had employed on the day before. He placed his men in two ranks, the first mounted and ready to make a dash upon any weak point in the enemy's line; the second dismounted and making capital practice at long ranges, with their saddles as a rest for the rifle. As soon as the front rank became too hardly pressed, they cantered to the rear, dismounted, and relieved the second rank.

When this had been going on for a little time the Zulus imagined that the terrible Buller and his men were flying from their onslaught, and thought the time ripe for a general advance. Meanwhile the action of the horsemen had brought the enemy within range of the Gatlings and Martinis of the square, which Buller and his men now rejoined. "Are the mounted men all in" asked Lord Chelmsford of General Newdigate.

"They are, my lord," replied Buller, who had got back and was imperturbably lighting a cigarette.

"Then give the enemy a round or two of shrapnel," said the commander, and a deadly hail was poured into the oncoming wave of savages.

It was a stiff fight for a while, the thousands of Zulus pressing on despite the many who fell, but at last they wavered, and the Lancers and other cavalry were sent out and routed and pursued them, and the Zulu War was practically brought to a close by the victory of Ulundi—a victory owing in no small degree to Colonel Redvers Buller.

Before Lord Chelmsford had been able to inflict this final blow upon the Zulu power, he had been practically superseded by the appointment of Sir Garnet Wolseley as Governor of South Africa, High Commissioner in Natal and the Transvaal, and Commander-in-Chief of Her Majesty's forces in Africa. Sir Garnet was indeed then on his way to the front, and Lord Chelmsford immediately after this victory resigned his command, while Sir Evelyn Wood and Colonel Buller also decided to retire—all prospects of much active military service being temporarily at an end.

In his official account of the Battle of Ulundi transmitted to the Secretary of State for War, Lord Chelmsford paid ungrudging tribute to the services which had been rendered by Colonel Buller, saying:

Lieutenant-Colonel Buller crossed the river by the lower drift to the right of our camp, and was soon in possession of the high ground on our front and the Undabakaombie Kraal. The object of Lieutenant-Colonel Buller's reconnaissance was to advance towards Ulundi, and to report on the road and whether there was a good position where our force could make its stand if attacked. I was also anxious, if possible, to cause the enemy to show his force, its points of gathering, and plan of attack. Lieutenant-Colonel Buller completely succeeded in the duty entrusted him.

Having collected his mounted men near Undabakaombie from the thorny country near the river, he advanced rapidly towards Ulundi, passing Nondwengo on his right. He had reached the vicinity of the stream Untukuwini, about three-quarters of a mile from Ulundi, when he was met by a heavy fire from a considerable body of the enemy lying concealed in the long grass around the stream.

Wheeling about, he retired to the high ground near Nondwengo, where he commenced to retire by alternate positions of his force in a deliberate manner. The Zulus were checked, but in the meantime large bodies of the enemy were to be seen advancing from every direction, and I was enabled with my own eyes to gain the information I wished for as to the manner of advance and points from which it would be made in the event of our force advancing to Ulundi. Though the Zulus advanced rapidly, and endeavoured to get round his flank, Lieutenant-Colonel Buller was able to retire his force across the river with but a few casualties.

He informed me of a position which, on the following day, my force occupied, and which subsequent events showed was admirably adapted for the purpose I had in view. I consider

PLAN OF THE BATTLE OF ULUNDI: JULY 4, 1879.

that this officer deserves very great credit for the manner in which he conducted this duty. That night the Zulus were moving about in large bodies, as testified by the sound of their war-songs, but they in no manner interfered with us.

"One of the finest episodes in this eventful war," Lord Chelmsford elsewhere said of Buller's reconnaissance on the day before the Battle of Ulundi.

While his superior officers were giving him due meed of praise, our hero himself was not neglectful of those who fought under him, as we find from his report made to Lord Chelmsford as follows:

My task has been materially lightened by the undermentioned. . . . Captain Lord William Beresford, 9th Lancers, my staff officer, who came from India for the Zulu War, has been of immense assistance to me. Energetic and untiring, he is always at hand when wanted, while his marked gallantry in the field and his pleasant address secured the respect and ready obedience of the men.

Nor was the new commander-in-chief less definite in acknowledging the services which had been performed by the dashing leader of the Frontier Light Horse, for when Colonel Buller was about to leave Zululand, Lord (then Sir Garnet) Wolseley issued the following General Order:

In notifying to the army in South Africa that Brigadier-General Wood, V.C., C.B., and Lieutenant-Colonel Buller, C.B., are about to leave Zululand for England, General Sir Garnet Wolseley desires to place on record his high appreciation of the services they have rendered during the war, which their military ability and untiring energy have so very largely contributed to bring to an end. The success which has attended the operations of the Flying Column is largely due to General Wood's genius for war, to the admirable system he has established in his command, and to the zeal and energy with which his ably conceived plans have been carried out by Colonel Buller.

Lord Wolseley also wrote to Sir Evelyn Wood at the same time, saying:

You and Buller have been the bright spots in this miserable war, and I have felt proud that I numbered you both amongst my friends and companions in arms.

Before actually leaving South Africa for home the officers were feted and congratulated in several of the chief towns by the grateful colonists. On one of these occasions, when speaking at Pietermaritzburg, Lord Chelmsford said:

> I never would have believed it possible for any general to receive such assistance and devotion as I have experienced from my men. . . . It would be invidious to particularise individuals and services, but when I look back eighteen months two names stand out in broad relief—the names of Wood and Buller. I can say that these two have been my right and left supporters during the whole of my time in this country.

On August 5th Colonel Buller and his late leaders set sail from Cape Town in the steamer S. S. *German*, and reached Plymouth before the end of the month. Ten days after they had left the Cape Sir Bartle Frere, the High Commissioner in South Africa, bore ungrudging testimony to the value of the work performed by Wood and Buller, as is seen in his despatch to the Secretary of State for the Colonies:

> I cannot permit Major-General Sir H. E. Wood, V.C., K.C.B., and Colonel Redvers Buller, V.C., C.B., to leave this colony without venturing to call the attention of Her Majesty's Government to the political services rendered by these officers during the two years and a half they have served in South Africa. It is not my province, nor is it necessary I should say a word regarding the military services they have performed, and I have already brought to the notice of Her Majesty's Government the important bearing which the position of Sir H. E. Wood's column in Zululand from January to July had on the safety of Natal and the Transvaal; but I would try to call attention to the excellent political effects of the dealings of these two officers with the colonial forces and with the colonists in general.
>
> Up to 1878, there had always been among the colonists somewhat of a dread of the strict discipline which was, as they thought, likely to be enforced by a military officer were they to serve under him, and a great distrust of Her Majesty's officers generally to conduct operations against the Kaffirs.
>
> The feeling has now, I believe, disappeared among all who have served under General Wood and Colonel Buller. They have

shown he colonists that military officers can deal with volunteers as with their own men, and lead them to assured victory without sacrificing or risking more than is necessary in so doing. To the experience of their treatment of officers and men under them is largely due the readiness with which officers of the regular army are now appointed to positions in the Colonial forces in the colony, and the good feeling which obtains at this moment between the Imperial and Colonial troops now in the field in Zululand.

I would particularly notice the influence which both officers gained over their Dutch auxiliaries and the Dutch population of the Transvaal districts bordering on Zululand. I believe that whenever Sir E. Wood and his gallant second-in-command may serve again in the Transvaal, they will find all who served under them in Zululand anxious again to join Her Majesty's forces in any capacity that may be desired.

CETEWAYO AFTER THE WAR

CHAPTER 5

Buller and Amajuba Hill

It is scarcely necessary to say that on his return to England Buller was one of the heroes of the hour. When the steamship S. S. *German* arrived at Plymouth on August 26, 1879, he received a cordial welcome home to his native county, and was surrounded by his Devon friends as soon as the ship came alongside. He travelled with his fellow-officers by Great Western Railway to Exeter, to the disappointment of those of his Exeter friends, who had arranged for a deputation to wait upon him at the other station for the purpose of presenting him with a congratulatory address. However, at the station at which he did arrive, he found the Rev. M. Swabey, the vicar of St. Thomas's, and a number of residents of the parish (of which the distinguished soldier is lord of the manor). In conversation with the vicar, Colonel Buller expressed the pleasure he felt at seeing so many familiar faces to welcome him home, and had the gratification of learning that he had been promoted to the rank of a full colonel.

Crediton, his birthplace and home, and Exeter, the capital city of his native county, were rivals in the desire to do honour to the returned Devonian, but though at first there was some slight jealousy between the two, it soon gave way, and each town performed its part in welcoming him. Although Colonel Buller had to go straight on to London, he was back in his native county within a week of his return to England, and a hearty Devon welcome was accorded him when he reached his native town—a welcome that was begun by the firing of a *feu de joie* of fog signals as the train bearing him ran into Crediton station.

This formed but a small indication of what was to come, for outside the station there was a regular procession waiting to convey the hero to his home half a mile or so away. The road was thronged with neighbours and visitors, while the whole route was made gay with a

142

display of bunting and with mottoes of welcome and congratulation to the returned officer. Opposite the entrance-gate of Downes a platform had been erected, and here Colonel Buller was received with an address of welcome delivered on behalf of the people of Crediton by the Rev. Prebendary Felton Smith. The address was worded as follows:—

To Lieut.-Col. Buller C.B., V.C.

Colonel Buller—As inhabitants of your native parish, many of whom have known you from your childhood, we joyfully avail ourselves of this occasion of your safe return from the arduous and harassing campaign in South Africa, to assure you of our hearty and affectionate welcome. We have watched, with the greatest anxiety and the intensest interest, your brilliant career through the whole of that campaign, and have hailed, with feelings of the deepest pride and gratification, the continuous and unanimous testimony of the British nation, not only to your undaunted bravery in action and self-devotion to the cause of duty, but to the consummate skill and unerring judgment, under circumstances of almost overpowering difficulty, which have rendered such signal and invaluable service to that army in which you were so distinguished a leader.

We feel assured that when the history of that war in which you have so lately engaged shall be written, the name of Buller will stand out as one of the most glorious upon its pages, and that that reconnaissance in which, with such strategical skill you selected the vantage ground on which that last decisive battle at Ulundi was fought, will ever be connected with your name, as contributing, perhaps in a greater degree than any action which could be named, to the virtual termination of the war. You have already won a distinction of which any British soldier may well be proud; and whatever other honours may be in store for you, we are quite certain that their outward symbols were never borne over a truer or nobler heart, or awarded to a braver soldier.

But while we feel, and are proud to feel, that your distinguished military career has established a claim by which the British nation at large will delight to number you amongst its heroes, we rejoice to remember at the same time that you are bound to us at Crediton by a closer and a dearer tie. You are returning today to the home of your ancestors, a home endeared to you by many memories which we cannot enter into, but we are sure that amongst the many endearments which cling in your case to that word 'Home,' there will be none more powerful in your mind than that which is afforded by the conviction that you are here surrounded by the loving hearts of friends and neighbours, who are proudly conscious that a reflected honour has fallen upon them, from the glory which attaches to you.

We know that it would be selfish in us to wish you to sacrifice the brilliant prospects which seem surely to await you in the career which you have chosen, for the sake of taking up your residence permanently amongst us, though we cannot help looking forward to the time when Downes shall be no more the mere remembrance of one whomever thus we love to think of, but the settled home of another of that name, which in the person of your beloved and lamented father, was significant of all that was loving and kind and sympathising.

To that home we this day bid you a hearty welcome, and we earnestly pray that God, who has thrown His protecting arm around you in the hour of danger and in the day of battle, may continue your shield through life, may prosper you in all your ways, and when the battle of life shall be ended, may give you His crown of glory in the life to come.

By desire of the parishioners of Crediton.

C. Felton Smith, M.A.,
Vicar of Crediton.

Having listened to his praises, always an uncomfortable position for a brave man, Colonel Buller had of course to acknowledge the very hearty welcome which was accorded him, and in doing so in a short, straightforward speech, insisted as he has always done upon the great services performed by the soldiers generally—services which make possible the honours for their leader. We shall not have many occasions on which to record speeches by the great soldier, so will give this and the one which he delivered a few weeks later at a great county banquet in full.

The bronzed soldier began:

Reverend sir, ladies and gentlemen, friends and neighbours, I thank you from my heart for the welcome you have given me this day. It is pleasant to return home at any time, but it is ex-

144

ceedingly pleasant to return home and receive such kind words and such marks of appreciation from those among whom you have been brought up, and from those you have known from childhood. With regard to what you have said about myself, I can hardly speak. I feel I have to thank you for many reasons for your reception today. I can never forget all that you have said on this as on one previous occasion, as to my family, and I can only assure you that if it should please God to allow me to settle here, it will be my earnest endeavour to walk in the footsteps of my father.

The reception you have given me today is more than a reception to an individual, for I cannot but think that in giving me this welcome you are also thanking those men to whose energy and courage I am indebted for being here today. I have seen in the newspapers adverse comments on the men who have been assisting the British troops in South Africa. I can only say this, that I have been living amongst them for eighteen months—volunteers and yeomen such as I see around me today, men who came forward in defence of their hearths and homes—and I can assure you that it would have been impossible for anyone to have had to do with a more gallant or more devoted body of men.

I feel that in receiving me this day you are thanking those men whose services have placed me where I am. In conclusion, I beg with my whole heart to thank you one and all for the great kindness you have shown in giving me such a welcome.

Lusty Devon cheering greeted the gallant officer's words and then the horses were removed from his carriage and willing hands drew it up the drive to the door of Colonel Buller's home.

A month later it was not Crediton only, but representatives of all parts of Devonshire, that met together to welcome home and do honour to the latest addition to the long roll of Devon worthies. It was on October 2nd, that a grand banquet was given to the popular soldier in the Victoria Hall, Exeter, under the presidency of the Duke of Somerset, Lord-Lieutenant of the county. Between four and five hundred ladies and gentlemen sat down. After the repast and the usual loyal toasts came the toast of the evening, in proposing which the Duke of Somerset asked the company to drink the health of "Colonel Buller, our guest, and a Devonshire man."

In reply, Colonel Buller made a speech which is marked at once by such characteristic modesty in the acceptance of praise, and has one or two such pertinent autobiographic touches that no apology is needed for quoting it at full now, just twenty years after it was delivered to an enthusiastic and admiring audience of the speaker's fellow-Devonians. When the applause with which his appearance was greeted had died away the hero of Inhlobane and Ulundi spoke as follows:—

I have first to endeavour, and it can only be an endeavour, to express to you insufficiently my thanks for the very kind manner in which my name has been received, and also for the magnificent testimonial you are giving me as a memorial of your kindness. The proceedings of this day will be always present in my memory. I shall always recollect them with the deepest feelings of gratitude and friendship. At the same time, I must say that I face you with a certain feeling of unworthiness. Had this war been a war of the older days, possibly I might have done ten times more than I have done, without any notice being taken of it.

I cannot help remembering that in the old days the general was the central figure of the army. The public obtained their information regarding the doings of that army only through the general's despatches; communication was difficult, and they came home but seldom. The general was trusted faithfully through reverses, and when in the end he achieved success he reaped the greater part of the glory.

In these days' matters have changed a good deal. The able and the brave men who now represent the public Press in all parts of the world keep us soldiers in the full blaze of light, and send home the most rapid and graphic descriptions of all we are doing. They have their duty to perform as we soldiers have, and they do it. Their duty is to interest the public, and we cannot fairly complain that in order to do that properly they are obliged to avoid generalities and professional technicalities, and to (as it were) personify everything.

Every mail requires some striking word-painted picture to be sent home, a picture in which some individual shall be prominent. I will do them justice, and say that they are all so kind-hearted, they always try and make the best of everything, and the consequence is that from their descriptions the visible hand of him who is called upon to execute is always recognised, praised, and perhaps over-duly honoured, while the hidden brain which has directed that hand, which has thought and planned-out the execution, is either forgotten or overlooked.

Be this as it may, whether in olden days I should have got the credit given me today or not, it does not prevent my great gratitude to you and my deep appreciation of the reception given to me as a Devonshire man by my fellow-countrymen. Throughout the record of dangers bravely met and difficulties successfully overcome, which we call English history, whenever there is anything important to be done the names of Devonshire men come more or less to the front.

I can hardly say as much now as I did when I last returned from abroad, when, out of four officers of the executive Staff, three were Devonshire men. Yet in this war Devonshire men have taken a leading part, and many of them have done remarkably good work. In the column I was with one of our best guides, and certainly the man who knew most of anybody about that unknown Zulu country, who had been thirty-six years on the frontier, and was really the pioneer of civilisation there—was a Tiverton man. We have all heard of the distinguished Devonshire man whose name is connected with the defence of Rorke's Drift—Major Chard. And of the many things I saw well done in that war—and I saw a great many well done—there was nothing that impressed me more than the way in which the officers and men of the Royal Artillery stood to their guns on the 29th of March. Alone, outside their entrenchments—with their supports near them certainly, but still behind their entrenchments—these officers and men fought their guns against overwhelming odds, and, as I have said, perfectly in the open.

It was a sight any Englishman might be well proud of, and it was additionally pleasing to me because the officer commanding the battery, Major Tremlett, was not only a Devonshire man, but came from my own valley—in fact, he was a Crediton man. I could multiply instances which I know of Devonshire men having done their duty as Devonshire men always do; but there are two which occur to me at this moment as particularly appropriate to mention.

I was passing through Maritzburg in August last year. The regiment I was commanding wanted a few recruits, and so many offered themselves that I had a good deal of difficulty in selecting them. I asked some ten or a dozen their names. The second man told me his name was Vinnicombe. I said, 'That's good enough for me, you come from the right end of England, at any rate.'—'Well,' he replied, 'I come from Devonshire.' And he was good enough for me. He stayed with me throughout the war, he was one of the very best men I had, and I had the greatest pleasure last week in writing to his mother to tell her that the queen had been pleased to give him one of the most valuable decorations a soldier can receive—the medal for distinguished service and gallant conduct in the field. I think I knew most of the Devonshire men with me; but I have found out a new one today. I mean Major Walsh, of the 13th Regiment, one of the most gallant officers in the field.

But there is one whom I must mention, last, but certainly not least; one who, if not a Devonshire man, Devonshire has more right to claim than any other county. I allude to Sir Evelyn Wood. His character is known to the world, and is beyond praise from me; but still I think I may say as a friend—and he has given me the right to call him 'friend'—that in Sir Evelyn Wood's character there is one thing which, above all others, I have learnt to wonder at and admire, namely, the manner in which he has been able to combine the most extreme resolution with the utmost kindness of heart. I don't know anybody with a kinder heart; in fact, I don't believe he ever did an unkind action, except, perhaps, he may have done a rather unkind one to me just now. Speaking so immediately before me on the same subject, he has, to a certain degree, taken my speech out of my mouth; and I, perhaps, owe him one for that.

But at the same time I cannot help rejoicing that he should have so done, and I know how grateful he, as a generous, kind man, must have been to have the first opportunity of bearing testimony to the many gallant deeds and many brave actions which have been done by men under his command, many of which, alas! were paid for by the actors' lives. I, too, feel grateful that so noble a theme should have fallen into the hands of one who is far better able to deal with it than I am. Sir Evelyn Wood has dealt broadly with the actions of the whole of the regular troops under his command.

He has also fully—I trust you will all agree with me here—fully exonerated the Flying Column to which I had the honour to belong, from the accusations of cruelty brought against the men composing it, and he has left me nothing new to deal with except, perhaps, what I may call the political side of the question. Now, I have been warned by the noble president that I must not touch the political side.

Well, soldiers have nothing to do with politics, and I think the less they know about them the better. But, at the same time, any workman does his work better when his heart is in it, and when he feels it is a good work; and I must say that war, which is a disagreeable thing to have anything to do with at any time, is rendered less repulsive to the actors in it if they can believe the war in which they are engaged is a right war. Now I am certain that when the history of the Zulu War comes to be written nobody will doubt that it was a righteous war. It was a war of civilisation against barbarity. No one who has ridden, as I have often done, across the valleys on the Natal and Transvaal side of Zululand, and seen what a beautiful, smiling country it is, a well-settled, fertile country, as it was up to two years ago, and tolerably thickly populated, can fail to believe that the whole of that country is meant to be a settled country in which men may live in peace and safety.

But before this war they could not do so. Early in the year, before the war was declared, I was riding along what was then our border, and I passed dozens of burnt-down and deserted farms. One particularly struck me, and I asked a Dutchman who was riding with me whose farm it was and why it was deserted? He said that poor Beestor was fond of his farm, and I noticed that the house was well built, that the cattle enclosures were well built, that there were plenty of fruit-trees and flowers, and that it was evident that a great deal of money had been laid out on the farm. I asked why poor Beestor had left, and my companion said he could not stay, the Zulus annoyed him so. I asked, 'What do you mean by annoying him?' He replied that they would come and drive his cattle away, and when he was away looking for them would sit on the fence sharpening their *assegais*, and tell his wife he would never come back again, and that they would kill her in the evening.

On one occasion my companion told me they said they came to hunt, but, instead of hunting, they stabbed this man's sheep and goats. Well, it has been said that the Zulus are a brave nation, who have only been defending their own country. I can only say that at the very beginning of this war they were intending to invade the part of the country I was in, and it was only stopped by General Wood attacking them and breaking up their column. But they did invade it afterwards, and our Flying Column had to trace them.

I must say I never can forget the feelings with which I saw their awful work, for the whole way was marked with slaughtered men, women, and children. I could not help thinking then, that had we waited and allowed such an invasion as that to be carried into Natal, how frightful the consequences must have been! It has been further said that the colonists of Natal have got up this war for their own ends and for their own profit, and have not attempted to assist us in any way, either in men, in money, or in hospitality.

I do not think that is true. As far as my own experience goes, I know it is not true. Among the many kind letters, I have received since I came here, congratulating me on my great and good fortune, I have received none kinder than a letter sent me by a lady, a colonist of Natal, whom I saw once, when, marching with some troops up the country, her husband met me on the road, and, much to his good wife's astonishment and annoyance, brought me in to partake of a breakfast she had not prepared for me. That lady wrote to me the other day, congratulating me, and saying how very pleasant it was to find that people whom she had known had got back safely from the war. When I tell you that this lady's own husband was slaughtered at Isandhlwana, and that her brother was one of my bravest lieutenants, you will imagine what her feelings must have been when she read in the papers that Natal had done nothing to assist in the war.

I hope that it will not be thought that I have dwelt too much upon this subject, but it is one upon which I feel deeply. When I recollect what the men are with whom I have been associated so long—when I remember that whatever I may have done is due to the assistance of men mostly colonists, men of whom any country in the world might be proud—knowing as I do that in whatever I may have done I have been assisted by these men, I cannot help feeling that those who have borne with me all the difficulties and dangers of the war have a right to an equal share with me in the honours and the kind words you are good enough to bestow upon me today. I should not feel that I had done my duty to these men who have served so gallantly with me if I had not taken this opportunity of vindicating their character and conduct from the unjust imputations that have been brought against them.

I ask you now, therefore, to let me feel that the praises, the kind words, and the honours you have bestowed on me today are offered equally, and belong equally, to those men who gained for me the renown I now enjoy. Then I can, as I do now, thank you with my whole heart.

It is pleasant to read this speech and find the brave man trying to lessen the importance of his own achievements, and to explain away his position as being more or less foisted upon him by the war correspondents; it is also extremely interesting, and especially at the present juncture, to recall his cordial words of praise for the Colonial horsemen whom he led to such dashing victories. The heroes of the Zulu War were indeed feted on all hands, and Buller came in not only for his share of general admiration and applause, but also for his due meed of praise from the commander of the British forces. Sir Evelyn Wood, too, never tired of recounting the good qualities of his able and brave lieutenant. He said, at a City banquet:

You have all heard of the valour of my right-hand man, but I alone, perhaps, can realise the full value of his services. Careful of his men's lives, reckless of his own, untiring and unflinching in the performance of duty, we owed much of our success to his brilliant leadership of our mounted men. To his devoted friendship I owe more than I can express. Men learn to know each other well in active service, and I have not known a better friend, nor a better soldier, than Redvers Buller.

Immediately on his return, as has been stated, Lieutenant-Colonel Buller was promoted to the rank of full colonel, and was further honoured by being appointed *aide-de-camp* to Her Majesty the Queen, while his personal bravery was to be familiarised to all men by the honourable initials, "V.C." being ever afterwards associated with his name, to show that he had gained the coveted honour of the Victoria Cross "for valour" shown in battle. That he merited that honour as but few have done we saw in following his doings during the war.

In 1880, he was appointed Quartermaster-General of the North British District, but did not hold that official position for long, as early in the year following, we find him again in South Africa. The Zulu troubles had been finally settled, and Sir Garnet Wolseley had made a peace. Troubles had, however, been simmering in the Transvaal, and these at length broke out in open revolt on the part of the Boers in December, 1880, when Colonel Anstruther's column was almost annihilated on the way to Pretoria. The prospect of further fighting attracted Colonel Buller to the Colony where he had already covered himself with honour, and shortly after the war broke out, he became Chief of the Staff of Sir Evelyn Wood, when that officer succeeded to the command of the unfortunate Sir George Pomeroy Colley.

Much has been heard in connection with General Buller's command in the war against the Transvaal Republic of the cry, "Remember Majuba," and indeed that terrible tragedy is little likely to be forgotten in England. Here briefest mention must be made of the tragedy, because it belongs to a story about Sir Redvers Buller which, if not true, is at least *ben trovato*. Although recounted with great circumstantiality as having been heard from Sir James Sivewright there are in it some doubtful elements.

Sir George Pomeroy Colley, who was Commander-in-Chief and Governor of Natal, suffered one or two serious reverses at the beginning of the war—in the same district as that first attacked by the Boers eighteen years later—and at the end of February, 1881, having marched a small force to the top of Amajuba Hill in the extreme north of Natal, was surrounded by the enemy and killed, his entire force being destroyed. The story runs that Colonel Redvers Buller, then acting as military secretary to Sir Leicester Smythe, Commander-in-Chief at the Cape, was visiting Mr. (now Sir) James Sivewright, then General Manager of the South African Telegraphs at his residence in a suburb of Cape Town, and was in unusually low spirits. His host rallied him on his quiet mood, when the officer confessed to feeling particularly anxious just then as to the course of the war in Natal.

Mr. Sivewright was as much astonished at the reason for it as he was at the mood, and argued that though Colley had suffered twice at the hands of the Transvaal *burghers* under Joubert, he was well able not only to hold his own, but to give a good account of himself, and to make the Boers suffer for their temerity in invading British territory; while, if required, was not Sir Evelyn Wood hurrying to the front with reinforcements?

Colonel Buller admitted this, but still felt that there was grave reason for anxiety, and argued:

Does Sir George Colley know this African ground as we know it? He may be tempted to go up one of those infernal hills. Very well, he'll climb one of them, but not really get to the top; or, if he does get there, he won't understand that the top's no use unless you know which ridge to guard. And, again, I ask you, does he know our African hills?

His host then suggested that they should drive into Cape Town and get into telegraphic communication with the camp at Mount Prospect—a suggestion which Buller cordially seconded, for in his gloomy mood, with a kind of prescience of coming danger, it was a great thing to be up and doing. They proceeded at once to the office, where the head of the Department soon got into communication with the camp, and received what he considered reassuring news—that Sir George Colley had moved out in force on the previous day, and was then understood to be in command of the Boer position, the enemy having probably retreated. Still Colonel Buller did not feel in any way satisfied, but rather the reverse, saying:

You'll see, it's the very thing I told you. Colley has gone up some mountain. He'll think he commands the Boer position, but he won't. It takes an African to do that. Please God the Boers have been bluffed and have bolted.

They went back to Mr. Sivewright's house to lunch, but during the afternoon the despondent Buller insisted upon returning to the town to learn if any news had come through. His host again accompanied him, and on their way, they met an official with a message for Mr. Sivewright. Impatiently Colonel Buller tore it open and read the fatal news that Sir George Colley had taken up a position on Amajuba Hill, had been stormed by the enemy, and he and his staff and most of his men were killed and the rest made prisoners!

For a moment the awful intelligence of the fate which had befallen his friend staggered Buller, but only for a moment was he overcome by it. Then he at once turned his attention to what was to be done in face of the calamity which had befallen the British forces in Natal. His mind was at once made up; he returned to Cape Town and going to General Smythe's quarters briefly explained what had happened. The general was no less shocked than Buller had been, and at once began considering what had best be done.

Buller is reported to have replied, with instant decision:

I'll tell you what we must do, sir, you must leave with me to-night to take over the command. You are senior officer in this country, and it is your right. We must catch the Boers at once. Here is Mr. Sivewright. He'll go to the Union Company and get you a small steamer, and we'll start at seven tonight.

The general raised objections, saying that he must at least see the governor. The masterful military secretary remonstrated:

But, as soon as you see Sir Hercules, he'll stop you. This isn't the time for 'waiting instructions from England.' We must go now. It is our—I beg your pardon, sir, it's my chance in life.

Finally, the general agreed, the steamer was secured, and the hour arranged for the departure arrived, but instead of General Smythe there came a note from him explaining that he had seen the governor, who had vetoed their little plan, and insisted on "waiting for instructions from England"! Thus it was that delays occurred, and at length, instead of prompt and sustained action against the revolted Transvaalers, a peace was patched up that gave the Boers pretty well all they wanted at the time, and that has now, after many years, led to another and bitterer war upon the same battle-grounds, and the officer who was denied the chance which he then wished to seize, has now gone out with full powers against the same enemy.

After Colley's death at Amajuba Hill the chief command in Natal devolved upon Colonel Buller's old friend and comrade-in-arms Sir Evelyn Wood, and Sir Evelyn promptly appointed the younger hero to be his Chief of the Staff, with the local rank of a major-general. Buller, although busily engaged in Natal with the onerous duties of his post, and having to be prepared for continuing the war at a moment's notice, so to speak, was not destined then to have any actual fighting with the Boers.

Sir Evelyn Wood was not allowed to "avenge Majuba," but acting under instructions from the Home Government had to enter into negotiations for a peace. It is understood Sir Evelyn Wood and General Buller had arranged for a double attack on Lang's Nek, the former working round and attacking from the Transvaal side, while Buller moved on it from Mount Prospect camp, whence Sir George Colley had made his ill-fated excursions against the enemy. However, it was not to be; the preliminaries of peace were arranged, and the ill-starred Convention of 1881, became an accomplished thing.

Storming the Inhlobane Mountain

When tidings of the disaster at Isandhlwana reached Brigadier Wood, then with the left column at the Zungi Mountain, he fell back on Fort Tinta, where he halted on the 25th January, and by the 31st had reached the banks of the White Umvolosi. On the same day he marched to Kambula Hill, where water was plentiful, wood easily obtainable, and where, accordingly, he formed an entrenched camp.

En route he had obtained full particulars concerning the Maglusini or Baglusini *kraal*, which he knew to be a muster place, and where were large quantities of Indian corn and other stores for the use of the Zulu armies, and towards which great droves of cattle had been seen driven.

Unless he proceeded with caution, and without ostentation, it appeared obvious to Colonel Wood, that the destruction of these magazines could be achieved only with a severe loss of men. He thus resolved to secure the same result by means of a raid of cavalry, composed of the dashing Frontier Horse, under Colonel Redvers Buller, and the Dutch *burgher* force, or troop of Piet Uys, 140 strong.

At four in the morning of the 1st February these troops left Kambula, and marched on the Maglusini *kraal*. This great centre of resistance lay thirty miles eastward of the camp, in the middle of a natural basin surrounded by precipitous hills.

Through these hills lay a pass, to hold which, and secure a retreat, Buller left thirty troopers, while, about half-past twelve p.m. he descended towards the *kraal*. As two other *kraals*, those of Umbelini and Ingatini, were in the vicinity, the greatest caution and secrecy in movement were necessary.

When the *kraal* came in sight, great herds of fine cattle were seen quietly grazing on the green hillsides. The *kraal* was very well built, and whether it held a strong force or not was quite unknown to

155

COLONEL REDVERS BULLER.

Buller's men, and this doubt added largely to the excitement of the raid. No alarm or suspicion had been roused as yet, and the double fact of the smallness of the force, and of its being composed entirely of mounted men, contributed to the success of the attack.

Throwing out a few vedettes, Buller felt his way carefully forward, and was ere long observed by some Zulus who were idling about, but who, on seeing his marksmen, fled to the hills, where they were speedily joined by others in some force. After exchanging a few shots, the troopers made a headlong dash at the *kraal*, which was captured almost without resistance, six men only being slain, and its huts, two hundred and fifty in number, with immense stores of grain, were instantly given to the flames. Then the troopers at a gallop, often using their swords as goads, gathered the cattle, to the number of 400, in one great herd, and drove them off in triumph, in the face of 300 men, who offered no opposition, either to the flankers or rear-guard.

Fort Kambula was finished on the 2nd of February, and armed with two guns, and before the 10th two more successful raids were achieved, under Buller, one into the Eloya Mountains, and another towards the Inhlobane Mountain, which resulted in the capture of 500 head of cattle, without any serious resistance.

While a new and stronger fort was being constructed, and occupied at Kambula, on the 15th Brigadier Wood made an attack on the great military *kraal* of a warlike chief named Manyanyoba, who had been killing and plundering in all directions in the valley traversed by the Intombe River. Prior to moving against this chief, who had been joined by Umbelini, known as the Swazi pretender, another turbulent warrior, who, in 1878, had expelled the German military colonists from their farms near Luneberg, several careful reconnaissances had been made, and from the local knowledge of a Dutch trooper of Piet Uys', Colonel Buller was enabled to carry out the instructions of Colonel Wood with success.

On the night of the 14th, at ten p.m., the force detailed for this service got under arms; they were composed of thirteen sabres of Buller's Horse, and fifty *burghers* under Piet Uys, 417 of Wood's Irregulars, eight Kaffrarian Rifles, and 100 Luneberg Natives. In profound silence, without lights, bugles, or other accessories, they moved off to the bush, not even a scabbard being permitted to clink; and the single gun which accompanied them had its wheels bandaged with strips of raw hide, for the double purpose of muffling their sound, and protecting them from the sharp rocks and boulders amid which lay a portion of the route.

The bright moon rose, and by its silent light they crossed the river at a ford, and got quickly into the bush, without being heard or seen by the occupants of some adjacent villages. A two hours' brisk march brought them to an open plain, traversed by a watercourse, through which they rode, and just as the grey dawn stole quietly in, the gun was got into position, and Buller gave the troopers their final instructions. Before them rose a range of mountains that averaged 1,000 feet in height.

This range ran along the valley leading to the smaller *kraals* in the distance. Half the cavalry were now sent away by Colonel Buller to the left, with instructions to gain the bush, and wait dismounted, until the shells were heard. They were then to dash forward at a swinging canter, and cut off the cattle seen to be feeding on the slopes, which manoeuvre, if carried out, would drive them into the hands of Piet Uys and his men posted on the right. Just as the sun began to appear above the horizon, the gunners managed to hit off the range to a nicety, and the second shell crushed and burst right into the centre of the interior circle, where the cattle are placed at night, and which is usually surrounded by the beehive-shaped huts in which the Zulus live.

The sudden explosion of these dreaded and—to them—inconceivable missiles caused the wildest commotion instantly in the *kraal*; flames burst forth, and mighty columns of white smoke began to ascend from it; amid these, dark figures were seen rushing about, and yells of men mingled with the bellowing of terrified oxen.

As Buller's Horse dashed forward on the *kraal*, the male occupants fired a ragged volley, and fled up the steep rocks, where no cavalry could follow them, and from whence they opened a file firing. The fighting and collection of cattle lasted about half an hour; of the Zulus, 34 were shot, and our losses were two killed, three wounded, and one missing; but 400 head of cattle and two large flocks of sheep and goats, were brought off by Colonel Buller, whose men got safely into camp at Kambula, after having been in the saddle for about nine hours.

On the same day a force under Colonel Rowlands, CB., late of the 34th Foot, and one of the nine officers "specially employed," was also engaged. That officer had been ordered to join Brigadier Wood, with a mixed force, composed of 103 Transvaal Rangers, 15 Boers, 240 of Fairlie's Swazis, and 75 Vos' Natives. While marching on the road from Luneberg to Derby, where a wing of the 80th was entrenched with two guns, Rowlands found the Talia Mountain occupied by the enemy, who manned the rocks and caverns on its southern side.

He attacked with only partial success, killed seven Zulus, and captured 197 head of cattle. After another affair on the 20th at the Eloya Mountains, Colonel Rowlands and his men started for Pretoria, as the attitude of the Boers in the Transvaal had become menacing, and then all the troops in the Luneberg and Derby district were placed under Brigadier Wood's command.

These and a few other petty movements, preluded what was known as the disaster on the Intombe River—an event somewhat similar to the calamity at Isandhlwana, though, fortunately, less in magnitude.

Luneberg was at this time occupied by five slender companies of the Both (Staffordshire Volunteers) under Major Charles Tucker, who had served in the Bhotan Expedition in 1865. He had also with him for a term Schembrucker's Kaffrarian Rifles, a corps raised from the survivors or descendants of the German Legion settled in British Kaffraria after the Crimean War, but they had now gone to join Wood's column at Kambula. Supplies for the garrison at Luneberg were being forwarded from Derby, and as twenty waggons laden with various stores were known to be on the road on the 7th of March, a company of the 80th under Captain David B. Moriarty, who had served with

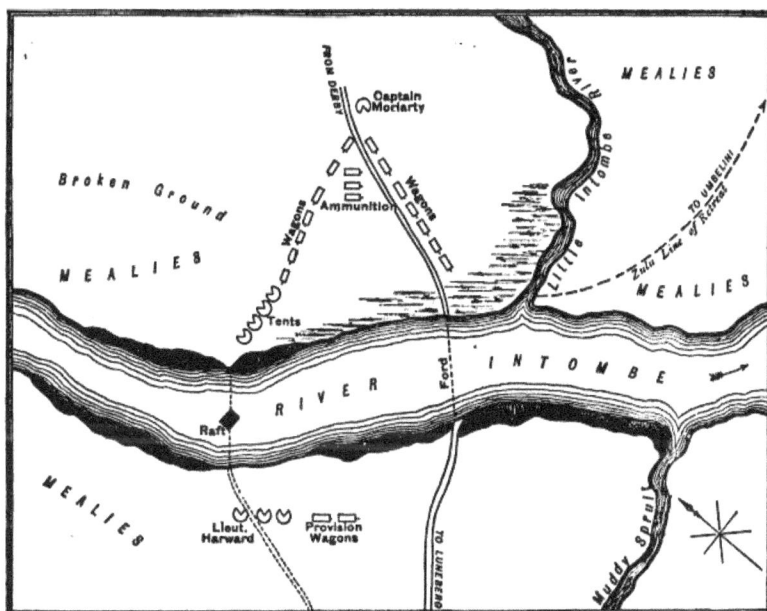

PLAN OF THE DISASTER ON THE INTOMBE RIVER (MARCH 12, 1879).

the 6th Foot in the Hazara campaign of 1868, was ordered to march from Luneberg, to meet and escort the convoy, which had arrived at the ford on the Intombe.

At first only a portion of the waggons of the convoy came, but with these the construction of a V-shaped *laager* was begun, resting on the river's bank. The situation was perilous, owing to the vicinity of a *kraal* belonging to Umbelini, the notorious Swazi freebooter, who had given much trouble of late.

The last of the convoy did not arrive till the 9th of March, when the waggon *laager* was completed, the flooded state of the Intombe rendering its passage impracticable. More rain fell; the river remained swollen, and on the 11th, when Major Tucker, full of anxiety, visited Captain Moriarty's company of seventy-one bayonets, he found it encamped on the bank, waiting for the water to subside.

> Major Tucker, on inspecting the arrangements for defence, considered the waggons too far apart, and objected to the space left between the last waggon of the *laager* and the river bank, but did not order any change to be made. (Report, Intelligence Department.)

On that day it was reported by the native waggon drivers that Um-

159

belini's people were gathering in arms. The camp has been described as being "pitched in a most dangerous position, with its face towards some high ground, covered here and there with dense bush, while its rear was resting upon the swollen river, across which Lieutenant Harward and thirty-four men were posted. No particular precautions appear to have been taken, excepting that a sentry was posted about fifteen paces from the front of the camp, on the Derby side," according to one account; or, according to another, with the exception of a guard stationed on each bank, each furnishing two sentries, but no pickets, the force being probably too slender to provide them.

On the morning of the 12th, at half-past four, while a thick haze rested on the swollen river, a shot was heard from the unfortunate sentry, while he shouted, mechanically, "Guard, turn out!" at a time when the officers and men on both sides of the river "were lying asleep and undressed." The shot and call made all stand to arms, for which there was barely time, as a force of 4,000 Zulus led, it is said, by Umbelini, was upon them!

Lieutenant Harward placed his thirty-four men under cover of a solitary waggon on his side, and made what dispositions he could to fire on the enemy's flank, while amid the dim light and gauzy mist, the whole valley could be seen swarming with dark-skinned savages, who at once surrounded the waggons, and *assegaied* the soldiers, in some instances ere they could leave their tents. The butchery—for it was no fight—was soon over, since all was confusion in a moment

Captain Moriarty was killed just as he left his tent, sword in hand, and his detachment on the left bank, being completely surprised, could offer no resistance to an attack so sudden and overwhelming.

The party on the other bank, taking advantage of the cover afforded by the waggons and also by some ant-hills, near the Intombe, opened a close fire on the Zulus, but failed to prevent 200 of them from crossing.

Lieutenant Harward, who commanded the party on the right bank, ordered his men to fall back on a farmhouse in their rear, and mounting his horse, galloped off to Luneberg for aid, leaving his handful of men to struggle as best they could without an officer to lead them.

Meanwhile, Colour-Sergeant Anthony Booth, of the 80th, did what Harward should have done. He rallied the few men who survived on the south bank of the river, and covered the retreat of fifty soldiers and others. The commanding officer of the 80th reported that, but for the coolness and bravery of this non-commissioned officer, not a man would have escaped with life; and so, Sergeant Booth was awarded the Victoria Cross.

The Zulus followed his party, consisting of only ten men, for three miles, but so bold was the front he showed, that he held them in check and retired without further loss. His resolute valour secured the escape of several fugitives from the left bank, who were without arms and some without clothes, and who were now in headlong flight for Luneberg.

Major Tucker, on receiving the report of Lieutenant Harward, started at once with a small mounted party for the Intombe, followed by 150 bayonets of the 80th, and on his arrival found that the Zulus had retired, carrying off with them the whole of the oxen, small-arm ammunition, rifles, blankets, and every scattered object of value, though, curiously enough, the waggons were only half pillaged.

Of the twenty-one men of the 80th, posted on the left bank of the Intombe, only twelve escaped, and some of those on the right bank also fell; making the total casualties 62 out of 106. Dr. Cobbin, two conductors, and fifteen drivers and leaders belonging to the Transport Department, also perished.

The dead were buried by Major Tucker, where they lay. They had all been stripped by the enemy.

Exaggerated details of this catastrophe renewed the terror which had been excited during the previous month in Natal, where a local print had the following passage:—

There are only 10,000 whites—men, women, and children—in Natal, and if 30,000 savages, skilled in military movements, and now effectively armed with the best that a British general's captured camp could yield, had come down flushed with victory, they could have devastated the land most thoroughly ... Her Majesty's forces are now, so to speak, sucked out of every garrison in South Africa, and drawn towards the scene of immediate danger. The gaps they leave have to be filled by the volunteer forces, and in many instances the individuals of the latter have forsaken business, family, and home, to do garrison duty for several months, wherever it may be required. More than that, every male civilian between the ages of eighteen and fifty, is now enrolled as a member of a *burgher* force to defend, if need be, the towns and villages which may be denuded of volunteers by the latter being sent to the front.

There were called into existence during the Zulu War, no less than thirty-six different corps of volunteers, horse and foot, making an average force of 9,114 men. When the Natal Native Contingent was first raised, ten *per cent* of the rank and file were supplied with fire-arms. Afterwards they were armed entirely with fire-arms, Martini-Henrys, Sniders, and muzzle-loaders. On the 20th February in the following year. Lieutenant Henry Harward, of the 80th Foot, was tried by a general court-martial, at Fort Napier, Pietermaritzburg, by order of the commander-in-chief, for abandoning his post at the Intombe in the face of the enemy; but the court recorded a verdict of "not guilty." The proceedings of the court were submitted to the commander-in-chief, who recorded the following minute:—

Disapproved and not confirmed—Lieutenant Harward to be released and to return to his duty.

And the animadversions that followed were ordered to be read at the head of every regiment in Her Majesty's service.

It was about the time of this catastrophe that Uhamu, a half-brother of Cetewayo, whom the latter kept prisoner in one of his *kraals*, escaped, and was brought by Captain Norman Macleod to Derby, accompanied by 700 followers. He urged that the Zulu Army was demoralised, that Cetewayo was unable to collect a strong fighting force, and he seemed to cherish the idea that his own submission might change the situation, and that he would be made king in place of Cetewayo, just as Panda was installed in place of Dingaan. For the time, he was sent to Utrecht

About the latter end of March, Colonel Wood received a letter from Lord Chelmsford, acquainting him with the steps he was about to take for the relief of Pearson's column at Etschowe, and giving instructions for a diversion that must be made on the 28th of the month.

Wood's force had been strengthened by Schembrucker's corps, 106 strong; Raaf's Transvaal Rangers, 100 men; and Weatherley's Border Horse, 61 troopers, with a squadron of 100 mounted infantry, under Lieutenant-Colonel J. Cecil Russell, of the 12th Lancers.

On the 26th of March he summoned to his tent Colonel Buller and Piet Uys, and told them that he had received information, that a great herd of cattle—the chief wealth of the Zulus—had been seen on the Inhlobane Mountain, about twelve miles distant from the camp at Kambula, from which it was quite visible. The hill was well wooded, full of caves, and was in fact a natural fastness; and as several recon-

ATTACK OF THE ZULUS ON THE ESCORT OF THE EIGHTIETH REGIMENT AT THE INTOMBE RIVER.

naissances had been made of it, the brigadier and Buller were familiar with its features. Captain Tomasson says:

> This mountain was deemed impregnable by the Zulus, it was a huge square mass with precipitous sides, a flat top, some four or five miles long, and of a good breadth. There was only one way up, which was hard and difficult, and at the other end there was a way down, but it was well-nigh impracticable. Possibly there may have been unknown cattle-paths down its sides.

Colonel Wood was aware that bands of Zulus guarding herds of cattle had been for some time lurking amid its rocky recesses, and that in compliance with orders from Cetewayo, these bands had been re-inforced by regiments sent from Ulundi, for the purpose of delivering an assault upon the camp at Kambula. Thus, to take the initiative and strike a decisive blow before more forces were concentrated, was now necessary, and would effect the diversion desired by Lord Chelmsford.

On the southern side of the Inhlobane Mountain there is an al-most inaccessible ledge or terrace, on which the dome-roofed *kraals* of the natives were built, but the summit, which could only be reached with the greatest difficulty, was uninhabited, and used as a place of safety for the cattle of the people who dwelt below.

The attacking force was to be furnished by the Mounted Infantry and native levies, operating against the mountain simultaneously at both ends of it. That sent against the eastern flank was to be the chief attack, while the other was to create a diversion and act as a support, but was not to assault if a desperate resistance was encountered.

The total of the mounted force was 495 men, according to Major Ashe (but the details of it differ), each furnished with three days' rations and 100 rounds of ball cartridge. All were picked swordsmen and marksmen. The horses were carefully inspected, and any that seemed faulty, were retained and others substituted for them, and all these animals were so well trained and docile, that many would come from grass when summoned by their masters' whistle.

The eastern reconnaissance was to be under Lieutenant-Colonel Buller, and the western under Lieutenant-Colonel Russell, both of whom were to send out scouts to watch for a Zulu Army, said to be advancing on Kambula. On the 27th, Buller marched from camp with 400 horse and some natives, 675 in all, and after a thirty miles' cir-cuitous route, bivouacked five miles south-east of the mountain; and about noon the same day, Russell, with 250 horse, a rocket battery, a

COLONEL WEATHERLEY.

battalion of Wood's Irregulars, and 150 of Uhamu's warriors, in all 640, after a fifteen miles' march, bivouacked four miles from the western flank of the mountain. In the evening the brigadier followed with his staff, including Captain the Hon. Ronald Campbell.

The night was damp and gloomy. The steep and precipitous Inhlobane could be seen in the gleams of the fitful moonshine, now in light, and *anon* in shadow, while the passing clouds seemed to foretell a day of storm.

Buller was for no more delay, and at half past three a.m., the word was passed quietly and quickly round for the men to stand to their horses, mount and march.

Under cover of the morning mist he reached the mountain, and ultimately, under the same friendly cover, the summit. Prior to this, the brigadier having been distinctly informed by Umtongo, the youngest of Cetewayo's innumerable brothers, that a Zulu Army was on the way from Ulundi, pushed on to make a junction with Colonel Buller and Weatherley and Piet Uys, lest they should be cut off.

The steep path by which Buller led his column was scarcely passable for mounted men, yet Captain Tomasson states that the Irregulars led up their horses by the bridle, and on arriving at the top:

The men scattered and fired at their foes below them on the

rocks. Captain the Baron von Sleitenkvon was here shot, as he was leaning over the edge of the hill.

He was a lieutenant of the Frontier Horse.

The firing on the summit of the hill could now be heard by the other column, which the brigadier ordered to push on, and as the ruddy sun was now up, a broken or bloody *assegai*, a battered shield, a dead troop-horse, and some Zulu corpses, could be seen here and there, indicating the line by which Buller had fought his way upward.

Most of the party with the brigadier had now dismounted, and, quitting their horses below a ledge of rock, ascended on foot. Wood himself leading his horse, with his staff and a small escort, was a little in front of Weatherley's men, when, at a short distance from the summit, a heavy and well-directed fire was poured upon them, flashing out from some dark crevices in the rocks above. Here Mr. Lloyd, Political Agent, fell mortally wounded while riding at a savage to cut him down, and the brigadier's horse was killed—disembowelled by a dreadful *assegai* wound

The shot which killed Lloyd tore one of Colonel Wood's sleeves to pieces.

As these and other casualties seemed to proceed from one cavern in particular, the brigadier ordered Colonel Weatherley to send a few bayonets to clear the place, at a time when he and his son, a gallant and chivalrous boy, aged only fifteen, were cheering on their men. As there was some delay in having this order obeyed, Captain the Hon. Ronald Campbell, of the Coldstream Guards, Chief Officer of the Staff, dashed forward, sword in hand, followed by Lieutenant Henry Lysons, Corporal Fowler, and three others of the Perthshire (later Cameronian) Regiment; but just as they reached the dark entrance, Campbell was shot through the head, after which every Zulu in the place was slain. He was the second son of John Campbell, Earl of Cawdor.

Colonel Weatherley and his men now moved on briskly to join Buller's force on the summit, while the brigadier and his escort descended to a ledge of rock where Mr. Lloyd lay. He was now dead, so his body and that of Captain Campbell were buried together near the foot of the mountain.

Colonel Buller, on gaining the high plateau—and to reach it more than one man had to clamber by clinging to vine creepers—saw how great was the area of the flat mountain top, where some 2,000 cattle were now collected, and that the Zulus who had been guarding them were dispersed. Accompanied by Piet Uys the colonel examined the plateau and the tracks by which a descent from it might be made, and of these there appeared to be three, *viz.*, that at the north-eastern end by which the ascent had been made, and two at the western end, both more difficult to traverse than the first, which, as it was secure from a flanking fire, Buller resolved to use for the retreat of at least a part of his force.

It was now the hour of nine a.m., and all seemed quiet on the summit, the Zulus having concealed themselves among the rocks and in caverns and crevices. Buller returned to the east end of the mountain, and sent Captain Barton, of the Coldstream Guards, his second in command, in search of Colonel Weatherley, with orders to return with him to Kambula by the route south of the mountain, which had been adopted on the preceding day.

Barton had scarcely departed on this errand when Buller saw a Zulu army, fully 30,000 strong, approaching the mountain from the south-east, looking, from the colour of their shields and the hue of their skins, like huge grey-speckled masses, moving amid the morning haze.

This army, the approach of which was known to Colonel Wood, who never could conceive it capable of compassing the distance it had marched in three days, was still about six miles distant; and it was calculated that the force on the mountain might thus have an hour's start

The retreat of that portion of the force now ordered back to the fortified camp at Kambula, was then so seriously threatened that two troopers were sent after Captain Barton with orders "to return by the right of the mountain," an expression by which Buller intended to convey the idea that he was to adopt the homeward route by the north, instead of the south, as at first proposed.

By this time the captured cattle had been collected by Raaf's Transvaal Rangers and Wood's Irregulars (two corps, about 138 and 460 strong, respectively), near the western extremity of the tabular summit of Inhlobane, and towards this point Buller and the men with him at once proceeded, in hopes that they would gain the support of Colonel Russell's force, which had been directed to that end of the mountain.

But mistakes had already occurred, and these led to another disaster. Had Wood's column, or portion of the attack, together with that of Weatherley, come on the scene of action in time to support the brilliant advance of Buller in the first place, all would have gone well:

But a delay caused by their missing the track, had enabled the

Inhlobane followers of Umbelini and Manyanyoba to hold their own ground until the arrival of the Ulundi Army. Buller did all that a skilled general could do to bring off his men with small loss; but from the nature of the ground it was, in this instance, impossible for cavalry to work with any degree of celerity.

Russell's force was now in position on a small plateau, about 150 feet below that occupied by Buller. Viewed from thence, the path upward seemed totally impracticable for horsemen, consequently Russell made no attempt to ascend.

As it was impossible to see, from the place where he was posted, what was occurring above, Colonel Russell—about seven in the morning—sent Captain Browne with twenty mounted infantry, to communicate with Buller's party on the upper plateau. Without opposition he reached it, and after conferring with Major Tremlett, R.A., and Major W. Knox Leet of the 13th Regiment, a veteran of the wars in India, he returned to report "that all was quiet on the upper plateau, but that the path was almost impracticable even for men on foot."

By nine a.m., Colonel Russell saw the approaching Zulus, and to all who noticed the rapidity with which they advanced, it must have been apparent that there was a decided prospect of all on the mountain being cut off and pitilessly slaughtered. He ordered his men to abandon some cattle they had collected and to secure their own retreat to the open country below. He sent the native troops back towards Kambula, and drew up his mounted men at the base of the mountain to cover the retreat of Buller, instead of joining Colonel Wood, for here some instructions would seem to have been misconstrued, and the latter officer had taken post at the eastern end of Zungi Mountain, six miles from the spot towards which Russell had hastened with his mounted men.

Meanwhile the Zulus were coming on, advancing, in a line of five contiguous columns, with a cloud, of skirmishers thrown out in front and both flanks, forming as usual, two horns and a centre.

The approach of the army was now seen by the Zulu inhabitants of the mountain, who came out of their hiding-places in increasing numbers and began to harass the movements of Buller towards the western end of the plateau. The difficulties of the descent became more evident than ever; no support came from Russell's party, and Buller had no alternative but to continue the perilous line of retreat to which he had committed himself.

The mountain side could be considered passable by horses only,

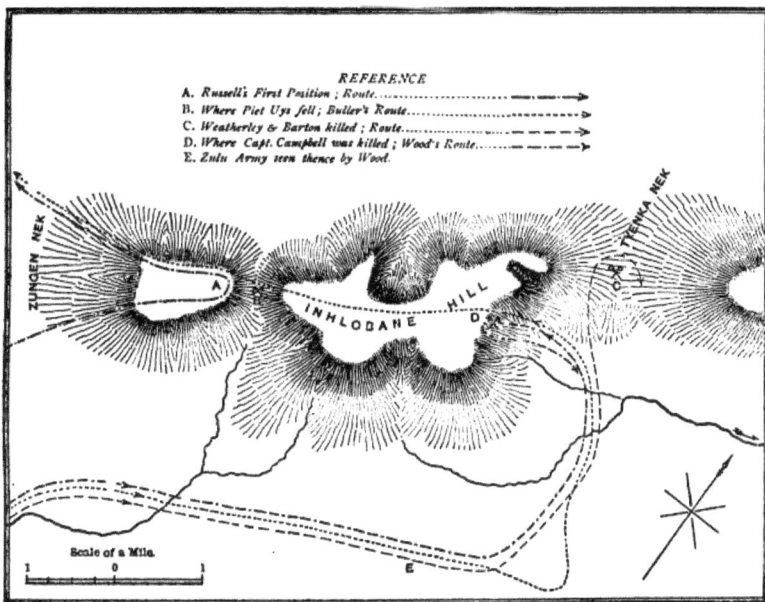

PLAN OF THE FIGHT ON THE INHLOBANE MOUNTAIN (MARCH 28, 1879).

by reason of the fact that the rocks of the encircling precipice here presented some appearance of regularity, and formed a series of ledges from eight to twelve feet wide, in which an insecure foot-hold could be obtained, the drop from one ledge to the next being about three or four feet.

How horses were got either up or down such ground, seems a riddle, yet such is the description of it as given in the Report of the Intelligence Department.

The native portion of Buller's force descended first, their rear being covered by the Frontier Light Horse, and now the dire havoc began. The Zulus of the mountain promptly occupied the rocks close to the line of the descent and poured a hot fire at point blank range into those who were helplessly endeavouring to get their struggling and scrambling horses over the almost impassable obstacles that barred their descent, and the casualties now became serious indeed.

In many instances the poor horses had to jump down three or four feet, then falling they broke their legs or necks, while the riders after discharging their carbines, became helpless, and were at the mercy of *assegais* thrust or launched.

Captain Tomasson says:

Save for the heroic efforts of Colonel Buller, it would have been extermination. Six lives he is known to have saved that day personally, and how many more by his orders and example, it would be impossible to tell Major Knox Leet of the 13th Light Infantry, serving with some native allies, brought out Lieutenant Smith, of the Frontier Light Horse, on a pack-horse—his own being shot—and earned the V.C. Some of the Light Horse kept, in some measure, the advancing Zulus back and enabled the rear-guard to extricate themselves.

An officer and sixteen men were lost, and here fell the gallant old Dutch farmer, Piet Uys, the leader of the Boer contingent—"splendid, manly, honest, simple and taciturn Piet Uys, whose father, uncles and cousins, fought and fell in the old wars with Dingaan." He was last seen with his back to a rock, standing across the dead body of his favourite grey horse, with six Zulus lying dead at his feet, his empty revolver in his left hand, a bloody sabre in his right, and two *assegais* quivering in his body.

At last the lower plateau was reached down that rocky way, strewn with bodies and splashed with blood. The force was now disorganised; many were dismounted, their horses having escaped their hands and fallen over the rocks, and if the fears which all entertained, of an immediate attack of the great army from Ulundi had been realised, no man would have escaped to tell the tale. No attack was made as yet, and Buller, who had been forty-eight hours in the saddle, and was severely contused by a bullet, rallying his men drew them towards the Zungen Mountain, unmolested save by the fire from the Inhlobane Zulus.

It would appear that Captain Barton, on joining Colonel Weatherley, proceeded with him towards Kambula, till they found themselves near the Zulu Army, which by this time had approached the fatal Inhlobane so close as to leave no outlet between its right flank and the mountain. From this position, a most perilous and critical one, they thought to extricate themselves by wheeling about and endeavouring to cross the Ityenka Nek, and obtain a safe line of retreat on the north. The passage to this was already barred on one hand by Zulus who had come down from the mountain, and on the other by a portion of the advancing army.

Desperate was the fighting now, as they attempted to hew out a passage through the holders of the Ityenka Nek, and to the valour and coolness, the devotion and heroism of Buller, it was due that any ever reached the camp at Kambula. With his own hand he covered the rear of the retiring column, charging again and again into the dense masses of ferocious Zulus, who were all athirst for blood and carnage; and not until he saw the last of his men out of that terrible gorge in the rocks did he take time to draw breath or think of his own safety.

All the Border Horse except eight troopers were slain. Captain Barton and eighteen of the Frontier Horse perished, with Colonel Weatherley and his son, a boy in his fifteenth year, a sub-lieutenant .Great were the slaughter and confusion, so that in some instances adjutants and sergeants had much trouble in making out the lists.

Major Ashe says:

> Nothing could be more sad than Weatherley's death. At the fatal hour when all save honour seemed lost, he placed his beloved boy upon his best horse, and, kissing him on the forehead, commended him to another Father's care, and implored him to overtake the nearest column of the British horse, which seemed at that time to be cutting its way out. The boy clung to his father, and begged to be allowed to stay by his side, and share his life or death. The contrast was characteristic—the man, a bearded, bronzed, and hardy *sabreur*, with a father's tears upon his cheek, while the blue-eyed and fair-haired lad, with much of the beauty of a girl in his appearance, was calmly and with a smile of delight loading his father's favourite carbine. When the two noble hearts were last seen, the father, wounded to death with cruel *assegais*, was clasping his boy's hand with his left, while the right cut down the brawny savages who came to despoil him of his charge.

Colonel Frederick Augustus Weatherley had previously served Her Majesty as a lieutenant in the 4th Light Dragoons (now Hussars), and as a captain in the Inniskilling Dragoons, under date 28th January, 1862.

So steady was the advance of the Zulu Army, and so dense their formation, that a broad tract of grass, over which they advanced, was completely destroyed by their bare feet. Brigadier Wood, after ordering Lieutenant-Colonel Russell to the Zungen Nek in the early part of the day, went himself about noon to this place—*viz.*, the low ground at the eastern base of the Zungi Mountain, and, finding that he was not joined by that officer and his force, he sent a fresh order, directing him:

> To move eastward from the point to which he had gone, and cover the retreat of the natives belonging to Buller's force, who

were suffering heavy loss at this time.

Before this order could be delivered, Russell, in consequence of a mistake in the term "Zungen Nek," had already taken up a position at the end of the Zungi Mountain, and ere he could push on to the assistance of the native troops they had been cut off, almost to a man, and his force reached Kambula about nine p.m., unmolested by the Zulu Army, which was worn out by its long and rapid march. The Zulu loss was estimated at 3,000, and Cetewayo was said to have been a spectator of the conflict. (*Daily News,*)

Heavy indeed were the casualties of the day. There were killed about fifteen officers and seventy-nine non-commissioned officers and men; one officer and seven men wounded. But the number killed was uncertain, as several were reported missing, among others Captain Robert Johnstone Barton, of the Coldstream Guards, and formerly of the 9th Lancers, whose remains were not found and identified till the 28th of May, 1880, by a small party sent from the Ityotyosi River by Brigadier—afterwards Sir Evelyn—Wood, K.C.B., and then accompanying the Empress Eugenie.

It would appear that Captain Barton had descended safely to the open country north of the mountain, and was endeavouring to make his way back to Kambula, but, having taken a dismounted soldier up behind him, he was pursued, and thus easily overtaken near the Monzana River by some mounted Zulus, who were pursuing him and

CAPTAIN THE HON. RONALD CAMPBELL.

other fugitives from the Ityenka Nek. Finding escape together impossible, Captain Barton and his comrade separated, and the latter, being unarmed, was slain at once; and Barton, whose revolver was out of order and thus thrice missed fire, was shot from behind and *assegaied* by the same Zulu who, fourteen months after, guided the party to where his remains were found undisturbed amid the solitude of the African *veldt*. Redvers Buller obtained the V.C.:

> For his gallant conduct in the retreat at Inhlobane, in having assisted, while hotly pursued by Zulus, in rescuing Captain D'Arcy, of the Frontier Light Horse, who was retiring on foot, and carrying him on his horse, until he overtook the rear-guard; also, for having, on the same date and under the same circumstances, conveyed Lieutenant C. Everitt, of the Frontier Light Horse, whose horse had been killed under him, to a place of safety. Later on. Colonel Buller, in the same manner, saved a trooper of the Frontier Light Horse, whose horse was completely exhausted, and who otherwise would have been killed by the Zulus, who were within 80 yards of him.

The V.C. was also given by Her Majesty to Lieutenant Henry Lysons:

> 2nd battalion, Cameronians (Scottish Rifles), and Private Fowler, of the same corps (then 90th), for having, in a most determined manner, advanced over a mass of fallen boulders, and between walls, that led to a cave in which the enemy were hidden. It being impossible for two men to walk abreast, the assailants were, consequently, obliged to keep in single file, and, as Captain Campbell was leading, he arrived first at the mouth of the cave from which the Zulus were firing, and there met his death. Lieutenant Lysons and Private Fowler immediately dashed into the cave, from which led several subterranean passages, and firing into the chasm below succeeded in forcing the occupants to forsake their stronghold. Lieutenant Lysons remained at the cave's mouth for some minutes during the attack, during which Captain Campbell's body was carried down the slopes.

Doubts have sometimes been expressed as to whether the Zulus always mutilated the slain—at least, beyond ripping them open. Of this they make a particular point, according to a Natal correspondent of the *Daily News*, in consequence of a universally prevalent superstition, that if an enemy is killed in battle, and his body afterwards swells and bursts, so will that of his slayer burst open alive. So intense is this belief of theirs, that at the attack on Rorke's Drift, after the fate of the day had been decided, several Zulus were seen to pause under a heavy fire, and deliberately rip up the few who were killed on our side, outside the entrenchment. Cases have been known in which Zulus, who have been unable to perform this ghastly ceremony, have committed suicide, rather than await what they conceived to be their inevitable fate.

www.ingramcontent.com/pod-product-compliance
Lightning Source LLC
Chambersburg PA
CBHW021105090426
42738CB00006B/517

* 9 7 8 1 9 1 5 2 3 4 0 5 6 *